Praise for this book

"Overall, I feel this is possibly the best work I have seen on this type of a dissertation. It is clear and concise as well as complete in mechanics." —Michael E. Cox, Ph.D.

"It seems to make writing a phenomenological study more accessible by offering pathways to students." —Dr. Akin Taiwo, King's University College at Western University, London, ON, Canada

"While this book conforms with others in the domain of phenomenological research it is superior in many respects: chiefly the author's sound knowledge transfer of philosophy to methods, the fit between conceptual basic assumptions and object of research study, and clarity without sacrificing complexity." —Maurice Apprey, University of Virginia

"The key strengths are the attempt to provide a systematic understanding of the process from A to Z with a specific focus on phenomenology. This text will be useful and versatile for student locked in to phenomenology." —Raymond Blanton, University of the Incarnate Word

Qualitative Research Methods Series

● ●

Series Editor: David L. Morgan, *Portland State University*

The *Qualitative Research Methods Series* currently consists of 56 volumes that address essential aspects of using qualitative methods across social and behavioral sciences. These widely used books provide valuable resources for a broad range of scholars, researchers, teachers, students, and community-based researchers.

The series publishes volumes that

- address topics of current interest to the field of qualitative research.

- provide practical guidance and assistance with collecting and analyzing qualitative data.

- highlight essential issues in qualitative research, including strategies for addressing those issues.

- add new voices to the field of qualitative research.

A key characteristic of the Qualitative Research Methods Series is an emphasis on both a "why to" and a "how-to" perspective so that readers will understand the purposes and motivations behind a method, as well as the practical and technical aspects of using that method. These relatively short and inexpensive books rely on a cross-disciplinary approach, and they typically include examples from practice; tables, boxes, and figures; discussion questions; application activities; and further reading sources.

New and forthcoming volumes in the Series include the following:

Qualitative Longitudinal Methods: Researching Implementation and Change
Mary Lynne Derrington

Qualitative Instrument Design: A Guide for the Novice Researcher
Felice D. Billups

How to Write a Phenomenological Dissertation
Katarzyna Peoples

Hybrid Ethnography: Online, Offline, and In-Between

Photovoice for Social Justice: Image Capturing in Action

Reflexive Narrative: Self-Inquiry Toward Self-Realization and Its Performance

For information on how to submit a proposal for the Series, please contact

- David L. Morgan, Series Editor: morgand@pdx.edu

- Leah Fargotstein, Acquisitions Editor, SAGE: leah.fargotstein@sagepub.com

How to Write a Phenomenological Dissertation

*In memory of Dr. Anthony Boone, who had a
brilliant mind and a gentle heart.
You have touched so many lives, dear friend.
Know that you will never be forgotten.*

1966 – 2018

How to Write a Phenomenological Dissertation

A Step-by-Step Guide

Katarzyna Peoples

Walden University

Los Angeles | London | New Delhi
Singapore | Washington DC | Melbourne

FOR INFORMATION:

SAGE Publications, Inc.
2455 Teller Road
Thousand Oaks, California 91320
E-mail: order@sagepub.com

SAGE Publications Ltd.
1 Oliver's Yard
55 City Road
London, EC1Y 1SP
United Kingdom

SAGE Publications India Pvt. Ltd.
B 1/I 1 Mohan Cooperative Industrial Area
Mathura Road, New Delhi 110 044
India

SAGE Publications Asia-Pacific Pte. Ltd.
18 Cross Street #10-10/11/12
China Square Central
Singapore 048423

Library of Congress Cataloging-in-Publication Data

Names: Peoples, Katarzyna, author. | Sage Publications.

Title: How to write a phenomenological dissertation: a step-by-step guide / Katarzyna Peoples, Walden University.

Other titles: Qualitative research methods.

Description: First Edition. | Thousand Oaks : SAGE Publications, Inc, 2020. | Series: Qualitative Research Methods series | Includes bibliographical references.

Identifiers: LCCN 2019046880 | ISBN 9781544328362 (Paperback) | ISBN 9781544328348 (ePub) | ISBN 9781544328355 (ePub) | ISBN 9781544328379 (eBook)

Subjects: LCSH: Phenomenology—Research. | Dissertations, Academic—Authorship.

Classification: LCC B829.5 .P3634 2020 | DDC 142/.4072—dc23

LC record available at https://lccn.loc.gov/2019046880

Acquisitions Editor: Leah Fargotstein
Editorial Assistant: Sam Diaz
Production Editor: Andrew Olson
Copy Editor: Diane DiMura
Typesetter: Hurix Digital
Proofreader: Caryne Brown
Indexer: Beth Nauman-Montana
Cover Designer: Dally Verghese
Marketing Manager: Shari Countryman

20 21 22 23 24 10 9 8 7 6 5 4 3 2 1

Contents

PART III: AFTER YOUR DISSERTATION

Chapter 6: Other Phenomenological Methods

Acknowledgments

Thank you to my doctoral students who continually help me grow as a phenomenological researcher. Without the honor of teaching and mentoring them, I could not have written this book.

SAGE and I would also like to thank the following reviewers for their thoughtful comments:

Maurice Apprey, University of Virginia

Raymond Blanton, University of the Incarnate Word

Michael E. Cox, Ohio Christian University

Dr. Joel Cox, Liberty University

Tracy A. Evanson, University of North Dakota

Nyasha Grayman-Simpson, Goucher College

Michael A. Guerran, Lincoln University

Dory E. Hoffman, University of South Carolina

Dr. Akin Taiwo, King's University College at Western University

Deborah Ummel, Université de Sherbrooke

About the Author

Katarzyna Peoples studied existential psychology at Duquesne University (Pittsburgh, Pennsylvania) and earned both her bachelor's and her master's in Psychology at Duquesne University before moving over to earn her doctorate in Counselor Education & Supervision at Duquesne University. She started working in the addictions field in 1999 and shortly after started relationship and marriage counseling simultaneously. Dr. Peoples currently works as a core faculty member in the Counselor Education and Supervision Doctoral program at Walden University. She has written books, book chapters, and journal articles on numerous topics related to counseling, teaching, and philosophy. Dr. Peoples also has an online marriage counseling and coaching practice where she offers video, text, and phone counseling.

Before the Dissertation

CHAPTER 1

How to Begin

Before beginning the phenomenological dissertation endeavor, one must first be sure that one's methodological choice is appropriate for what one aims to accomplish for dissertation. Is phenomenological methodology the appropriate method for the research questions proposed? Before moving forward, one must understand the purpose of phenomenological research and, more important, what one will need to understand and accomplish as a phenomenological researcher. Phenomenological research differs substantially from all other qualitative methods.

What Is Phenomenological Research?

First and foremost, philosophy is the foundation of this kind of research. Any student who aims to complete a quality phenomenological research dissertation will need to study philosophy. Students are commonly required to incorporate a theoretical framework of their choosing for dissertation work, but the theoretical framework for phenomenological research is always phenomenology. There are two main philosophies to study for choosing a fitting phenomenological method: Husserl's transcendental phenomenology and Heidegger's hermeneutic phenomenology. It is certainly fine to use a different theoretical framework but only as a secondary framework to phenomenology. More on this is presented in Chapter 2.

Second, phenomenological research is strictly aimed at understanding experiences as lived. Meaning-making is essential to phenomenological inquiry but only within the construct of experience. A phenomenological research study is used to answer the question, "What is it like to experience a certain phenomenon?" If this same question is posed to enough people in a certain situation, a researcher can analyze multiple experiences of the same situation and make certain generalizations of a particular experience. This sounds simple enough, but it is precisely the simple concept of studying ONLY experience that brings about confusion. In general definitions of phenomenological research, one might find some explanations that state that phenomenological research is used to study or understand people's perceptions or perspectives of any particular situation. While this explanation is technically true (after all, perceptions and perspectives are all parts of experience), it can mislead a beginner researcher when constructing research questions. Phenomenological questions (both research questions and interview questions) are limited to experiences and do not ask about opinions, perceptions, perspectives, or any other thoughts about a topic. Within an experience, a person makes meaning of that experience, has perceptions about that experience, and interprets that experience, but the experience is neither meaning, perception, nor interpretation. A participant may state, "I think my grandmother hates me." While the participant is experiencing a thought and perhaps a feeling, the experience with his grandmother is not present. Hence, this statement would be about a perception rather than an experience. A phenomenological researcher would first note that this statement is indeed important and relevant to the participant and would then ask the client to explain the content of an experience. "Can you give me an example of when you thought your grandmother hated you and what happened at that moment when you felt that way?" The participant can then give an experience to illustrate the perception. Perhaps the participant talks about an instance when Grandmother reacted in a certain manner that elicited the thought or feeling of "my grandmother hates me." This would communicate the experience instead of a perception and would enable the researcher to analyze experience only.

Feelings of participants are different from perceptions or assumptions within the realm of experience. Participants can discuss what their experiences were like as lived experiences, and they can also discuss how they felt during those experiences. Discussions about lived experiences make it possible for others to imagine those experiences in their minds and what they were like. Discussions about the feelings of those participants in those experiences would communicate what the people having those experiences were like. Both approaches would be acceptable in phenomenological methodology. A phenomenological researcher must constantly make this differentiation throughout data collecting, data analysis, and research writing.

Last, phenomenological researchers endeavor to make a phenomenon a "meaningful named reality" (Willis, 2001, p. 2). Something is meaningful in that it refers to the person who experienced a certain phenomenon. Through participants' vivid depictions of their experiences, phenomenological researchers construct a meaningful reality through data analysis. Phenomenological researchers pause and look at a phenomenon as the lived experience of some activity and illuminate its specific characteristic as experience rather than trying to turn it into an abstract structure and comparing it to other structures. Reality is always understood in terms of consciousness rather than some objective thing that exists completely outside of what we know or think. Hence, the aim of the phenomenological researcher is "to understand and describe phenomena exactly as they appear in an individual's consciousness" (Phillipson, 1972). Phenomenological researchers also aim to reveal their lived experiences as they focus on named phenomena and how they have an impact on their experiences. In the end, they are not concerned with generating abstract concepts or hypotheses but aim to bring together the objective and subjective dimensions of experiences as lived.

Purpose of This Book

Now that you have determined that phenomenological research is indeed the correct methodology for your dissertation, let me move forward to explain the purpose of this book and how it will help you complete a phenomenological dissertation from start to finish. To begin, it is important to note that this book is written in the simplest how-to fashion for novice researchers; it is in no way intended to be used as a rigid technique with no room for modifications. Phenomenology is about personal experience, and personal experience varies from researcher to researcher. Hence, so should your phenomenological method. However, this very notion of encouraged variation within phenomenological research is the source of much confusion for novice researchers wanting to complete their first phenomenological research studies.

Alterations within phenomenological methodology continue to increase, and with those alterations, more debates emerge on how to most effectively execute phenomenological research in practice. Confusion about how to conduct suitable phenomenological research makes this field difficult for dissertation students to grasp. Because of my experience as a phenomenological researcher and a professor guiding scholars in training through the dissertation process of writing a phenomenological dissertation, this text has evolved over time and is grounded by the many questions and concerns my students have had as they struggled through the process of writing their phenomenological research dissertations. My goal throughout this book is to give dissertation students practical answers on how to design a phenomenological research dissertation from beginning to end. It is no easy feat, but student frustration is not usually for lack of resources. From the experiences of my students, I have indeed found that the wealth of information on phenomenology and phenomenological research can be the stumbling block.

"There are so many bits and pieces scattered among several books, but nothing that is very thorough. I need a clear and thorough explanation of the different kinds of phenomenology research methods. Who are the key players for each type? Are all these philosophers connected to each other?"

In this text, I provide a step-by-step process on how to write a phenomenological dissertation. This guide is meant to be simple and rudimentary for the first-time phenomenological researcher. I believe this is the best place to start. Only after mastering the beginner steps can novice phenomenological researchers begin to excel in further writing and developing expert phenomenological research studies that encompass their individual groundings in the philosophical traditions. This text is not intended to reduce the richness or complexity of phenomenological research through a series of how-to strategies. It is, however, meant to be the simplest step-by-step guide a novice phenomenological researcher can access. The process of beginning and finishing a high-quality phenomenological research dissertation is most certainly attainable.

The front and center of this entire text are the many questions, frustrations, and eventual achievements of dissertation students moving through the writing of a phenomenological research dissertation. I asked several of my dissertation students to provide me questions they had about starting their phenomenological research dissertations, and they were eager to oblige. The confusion and frustration are surely valid. In fact, one student said, "I think your book is so needed and wish that it was already completed so I had it to reference as I do my dissertation."

In this book, I not only answer the above questions but answer them in a step-by-step guide mirroring the dissertation process. Doing a phenomenological dissertation for the first time is often daunting and requires skills and knowledge that are different from those taught in many university and college programs, which often tend to dominate training in qualitative methods.

"I feel dumb because I really only studied quantitative research in undergrad and graduate school. Is that normal? Should I already know how to do some of this?"

While this text is a step-by-step guide for the beginner phenomenological research student, it is not a rigid method with no room for modification. Readers should read this book as a set of guidelines and recommendations for getting started rather than a permanent prescription for all future phenomenological research. To that end, it is purposefully written in the most basic way so that readers can grasp practical techniques to use in their first phenomenological research endeavors. As in any research, and I would argue especially in phenomenological research, a person first carefully implements a tried and tested strategy, and with gained confidence deviation and expansion of process and method later materialize.

The most important thing to remember in phenomenological research is that philosophy is just as important as techniques. Dissertation students who are well grounded in phenomenological philosophy will only then be able to create distinct and acculturated data analyses. It is only through the personal understanding of phenomenological philosophy that researchers can create superior phenomenological research. This can be intimidating, especially for the dissertation student who has never read any philosophy. Phenomenological philosophy can be extremely complex and difficult to understand. Many students would rather skip right over it and get to the techniques of phenomenological research, but that is missing the point completely. One simply cannot do this research well without grasping key philosophical ideas. I believe everyone can understand phenomenological philosophy if it is taught in a straightforward way, and it is my hope that this book will be helpful in that respect.

Organization of This Book

This book is written for dissertation students, so it is structured like the dissertation: Chapters 1 through 5. After readers move through the chapters and finish with the end of the dissertation, I provide additional chapters that are written for future expansion of phenomenological research as well as to provide additional information about this research process. Readers are encouraged to read each chapter in order without skipping chapters. Since each chapter is written to parallel the dissertation, readers can simultaneously work on their dissertations as they progress through this book.

Part II: Writing the Dissertation
Chapter 2
Introduction and Literature Review

Literature Review

Even though the literature review is the second chapter of the dissertation, I address it in the introduction because students need to extensively review the literature on their topics before they can design their proposals. I guide students on how to develop a researchable topic and then explore literature, using a step-by-step system in the chapter. Because the length and focus of this book limit an extensive expansion of how to write all elements of literature reviews, I offer more resources on where students can attain more detailed guidance, should they need it, by providing a Suggested Reading section at the end of the chapter. Suggested reading sections are included at the end of every chapter to provide readers with further guidance without overwhelming them with too much information in this book.

Introduction

In writing the introduction, a dissertation student must properly introduce the study. In this section, I provide a model for writing a high-quality introduction for the dissertation. Within this section, I include important information on how to present a balanced summary of literature, how to construct a good problem statement and a high-quality purpose statement, how to create good phenomenological research questions, how to create a phenomenological theoretical framework, how to know whether the phenomenological method is appropriate for the proposed study, how to delineate between phenomenological terms and tensions like interpretive (hermeneutic) phenomenology and descriptive (transcendental) phenomenology, the role of philosophy in this type of research, and how to write information thoroughly and succinctly. I also briefly guide students in how to write effective Chapter 1 sections, such as Definitions, Assumptions, Limitations, Delimitations, Significance, and Summary.

Problem Statement

What makes a good problem statement? This is the primary question I answer for readers to guide them in developing a quality problem statement to substantiate their research study. The seemingly simplistic structure of a well-written problem statement is one of the most difficult for dissertation students to master, until now.

Purpose Statement

In addition to the problem statement, the purpose statement is the other most important statement in a dissertation. In this section, I will guide students on how to write this statement, providing scripts that will help illustrate an effective structure.

Theoretical Framework
....

Theoretical frameworks serve as lenses in phenomenological studies, and they are a consistent source of confusion for dissertation students attempting to write phenomenological dissertations. In this section, I present the two main theoretical frameworks that dissertation students can use to frame their phenomenological studies, namely the phenomenology of Husserl (for transcendental or descriptive phenomenological dissertations) or Heidegger (for hermeneutic or interpretive phenomenological dissertations). The use of additional frameworks to frame a phenomenological study (like feminist theory, for example) and how to construct it within a phenomenological framework is also explained here in a step-by-step manner. These are two of the most common questions students ask in constructing their theoretical frameworks:

1. Who are the foundational philosophers or theorists associated with phenomenological research?

2. How do I identify which is best for guiding my research topic?

Chapter 3
Methods

Phenomenological methods differ from the other qualitative approaches in a significant way, and the groundwork of philosophy is a large factor in this differentiation. In this chapter, I explain how to construct a good phenomenological methodology and how to analyze data in a step-by-step manner so that someone else can replicate the study by reading the methodology. In this discussion, I also include information on how to use sampling, how to collect data, the role of triangulation, journaling options, and representation of all information in figures and tables. Some of the questions asked by students about their Methods sections that I will address in this text are the following:

1. Which sampling methods work best for phenomenological research?

2. What are acceptable data collection methods and coding procedures specific to phenomenological research?

3. How do I ensure that my interviewees stay within the parameters of my "funneled" topic?

4. Is it OK to have someone else transcribe research interviews?

Validity and Reliability

In this section, I show students how to address issues of validity and reliability in their studies and how these steps differ from quantitative methods. I cover strategies that are both easy to implement and more difficult to implement for phenomenological dissertations. Strategies include triangulation, member checking, addressing bias, thorough descriptions, peer debriefing, auditors, and time spent in the field. Not all are necessary or practical, and I find that many of my students have described strategies in their dissertations that surround their intent to provide valid and reliable results that are not realistic. This section is one of great importance for students to read, and I guide them in writing this section of their dissertations more effectively and pragmatically.

Data Analysis

For the data analysis portion of this chapter, I guide students in constructing step-by-step data analysis procedures that fall in line with their theoretical frameworks. If students choose to use descriptive or transcendental phenomenology, their data analysis procedures will differ from those students choosing interpretive or hermeneutic phenomenological methods. The incorporation of philosophical groundwork within the analysis is unique to phenomenological methods, and I describe how to accomplish this step in detail. These are some of the common questions I will also answer for students about analysis that they have asked me:

1. How do I know I am starting the coding process right?

2. Is there a coding process that is easier to learn to help frame the data interpretation process?

3. What if I feel that I'm just making up themes? What if I miss themes?

4. When I am analyzing the interview answers about experiences, there will be several things brought up that may not be experiences but opinions or viewpoints. How do I determine which segments to focus on?

Using Software

Using software for data analysis can be a point of contention for phenomenological researchers. I introduce readers to the concerns and benefits of using data analysis software in completing quality phenomenological analyses. I also provide practical guidance on what software data analysis might entail should a student choose to use software as a tool.

Journaling

Students are most often confused with the decision of whether to journal and how to journal when analyzing their data or when they interview participants. The decision to journal may or may not be appropriate depending on the type of phenomenological study that is chosen. I discuss these differences and guide readers on how to journal appropriately (when necessary) for specific phenomenological methods, when journaling is appropriate, when it is not, and how the chosen phenomenological discipline will dictate journaling as a tool for addressing bias.

Interviewing

Phenomenological interviewing is different from other research interviews. Students often have questions about how to conduct appropriate interviews. In this section, I cover how to determine appropriate interview techniques, such as individual interviews, follow-up interviews, and focus groups.

Abstract

The proposal of the dissertation consists of the first three chapters. After it is written, it needs to be submitted for formal review, and an oral defense typically follows. Before submitting the first three chapters, a student needs to begin the document with an abstract, and an abstract is typically written last as it summarizes the document. In this section, an example of how to write an appropriate abstract is discussed.

Chapter 4
Results

A quality results chapter in a phenomenological dissertation differs from other qualitative dissertations in that it needs to be grounded in phenomenological philosophy. In this section, I show dissertation students how to clearly write their data analysis results, how to ground them in phenomenology, and how to insert the results of the data analysis back into the Methods chapter so that the steps of the data analysis can be easily tested for validity and reliability.

Presenting Findings

Students are often confused on how to display data in a purposeful way. Many times, they simply display the data they have instead of presenting their best examples and relating them back to their research questions. In this section, I provide readers with the best strategies to present their phenomenological research findings. I show them how to sufficiently report their data from the analysis to support their conclusions in the form of quotations from the transcripts and their researcher observations.

Connecting to the Theoretical Framework

Students do not often understand that their findings need to relate back to their theoretical frameworks, and in this section, I give them instructions on how to connect their findings to their frameworks effectively.

Going Back to Chapter 3

At this point, students will have finished their Chapter 3: Methods, but that is not really the case since they will need to now go back and insert relevant quotes from their Chapter 4: Results to better illustrate their data analysis steps. In this section, I guide them through this process and explain the importance of this step, which has much to do with ability to replicate the study.

Chapter 5
Discussion

One of the most impressive qualities of a comprehensive discussion chapter is the comparison of one's own results with the ones presented in literature. Dissertation writers should not simply discuss their thoughts on the results and note implications for future research. Indeed, these elements are included, and discussed in this chapter, but they are incomplete without a dialogue with literature. In this chapter, I show readers how to present a thorough phenomenological dialogue between data analysis results and the literature review.

Dialogue With Literature

In this section, I teach students how to write a dialogue with the literature. The importance of connecting their results with their literature reviews is covered in detail here along with some examples on how this might look in a dissertation.

Implications for the Field

Many times, students are still unsure about how to provide recommendations from their findings, specifically in the area of choosing which lived experiences apply. I give them specific guidance on how to identify the most important contributions of their research and help them write about how their findings contribute to what is already known in their fields as well as how to broaden and challenge current field knowledge.

Limitations

In this section, I explain that all research has limitations in the interpretation of findings. Readers are taught how to explicitly address the major limitations of their research along with their implications. Readers are guided on how to be selective, focusing on the most relevant limitations to their research findings.

Recommendations for Future Research

In this section, I teach students that research findings can have various implications that contribute toward such different areas as the development of theories or identification of content that requires future research. I show readers how to provide detailed outlines for future research based on their findings rather than writing about general suggestions. This is often a challenge for students writing phenomenological dissertations because they have difficulty identifying specifics from lived experiences.

Part III: After Your Dissertation

Chapter 6
Other Phenomenological Studies

Within the Western tradition of phenomenology, there are three major disciplines: transcendental phenomenology, hermeneutic phenomenology, and existential phenomenology. There also exist a number of phenomenological research methodologies that do not explicitly use Husserlian or Heideggerian techniques. In this chapter, I present some alternative phenomenological methods that focus on rich descriptions of lived experience and meaning but do not strictly adhere to these disciplines. Some of these methods are these:

> critical narrative analysis (Langdridge)
>
> dialogal approach (Halling, Leifer, & Rowe)
>
> Dallas approach (Garza)
>
> embodied lifeworld approach (Todres)
>
> interpretive phenomenological analysis (Smith, Flowers, & Larkin)
>
> lifeworld approach (Ashworth)
>
> lived experience human science inquiry (van Manen)
>
> open lifeworld approach (Dahlberg)

I also discuss existential-phenomenological methodology in more detail. This chapter is intended to help readers expand their viewpoints on phenomenological method. It is recommended that this chapter be used only after students complete their phenomenological dissertations using Chapters 1 through 5 and move on to complete future phenomenological studies.

Chapter 7
Creating Your Own
Phenomenological Method

I wrote this chapter for dissertation students so they could expand their viewpoints on phenomenological method even further and show them how to experiment with alterations in future studies. It is also recommended that this chapter be used only after students complete their first phenomenological studies, their dissertations, and move on to complete more phenomenological research as scholars.

REFERENCES

Phillipson, M. (1972). Phenomenological philosophy and sociology. In P. Filmer, D. Phillipson, D. Silverman, & D. Walsh (Eds.), *New directions in sociological inquiry* (pp. 119–164). Cambridge: MIT Press.

Willis, P. (2001). The "Things Themselves" in phenomenology. *Indo-Pacific Journal of Phenomenology, 1*(1), 1–12.

Writing the Dissertation

Introduction & Literature Review

Acommon misconception about phenomenological research is that the researcher begins the research without reviewing literature. Concerns about literature reviews span several topics with regard to the integrity of method. For instance, there is a risk of introducing or suggesting ideas to participants during the interview process as well as the concern of increased researcher bias. While these concerns are noteworthy about phenomenological research, it is unrealistic to assume that anyone will allow research to be conducted without a proposal, which highlights why the study is needed through arguments found in in literature. Students need to present why the proposed study is needed and present it against the background of what is known and not known about the topic. Hence, a thorough literature review is necessary in all research, including phenomenological studies.

When writing a review of the literature on a proposed research topic, students determine whether the specific topic is worthy studying. When the exact topic is deemed thoroughly researched, the literature review is useful in helping the dissertation student refocus the scope of the research study to an area that deems inquiry. A thorough research of the literature assures that a research topic can and should be researched. Even though the literature review is the second chapter of the dissertation, students begin this process first since an extensive review of the literature is necessary for developing a proposed research topic.

Beginning the Literature Review: What's Your Topic?

Before any steps are taken, a dissertation student must first specify a research topic to study. Topics can be general to start and will, most often, become more specific as the review of the literature progresses. Perhaps a student researcher proposes "the experience of stress on doctoral students in dissertation writing" or "the experience of being homeless." A few words are acceptable to begin the process of reviewing literature.

Literature Search Strategy

After students choose a general topic of study, they should find journal articles and scholarly sources related to that topic. Students can do this in many ways depending on their organizational styles, but one piece of essential advice would be to create an outline. What information is missing in our field that needs to be explored further? This is the beginning of the search. Students should write this at the top of the outline as the title. This title may change as literature review progresses, and students can expect to revise it many times as necessary. An outline of the literature review will allow students to stay organized, stay focused on the topic, and create a proper funnel effect.

Create an Outline

A good literature review should flow from broad to specific. By creating a funnel configuration, a literature review will move from establishing the importance of the topic (WHY this is worth researching) to the specific research questions (HOW the answers will be acquired). A funnel will allow students to frame their arguments with sufficient detail so that readers are able to follow the logic and sequence of all major points.

Literature review outlines serve as a preview tools that allow dissertation students to see their literature review plans at a glance so that they can revise them as needed. By looking at the outline, students will be able to assure that their literature review has a proper scope and direction as well as proper organization. Outlines will differ among students' organizational styles but should typically follow a structure such as this:

Title (main topic)

1. First Main Idea (*broadest or most general*)

    a. First supporting argument

        i. Evidence or example (include citations)

        ii. Evidence or example (include citations)

        iii. Evidence or example (include citations)

b. Second supporting point
      i. Evidence or example (include citations)
      ii. Evidence or example (include citations)
2. Second Main Idea
   a. First supporting argument
      i. Evidence or example (include citations)
   b. Second supporting point
      i. Evidence or example (include citations)
      ii. Evidence or example (include citations)

   . . .

3. 15. Last Main Idea (*most specific to research question or questions*)
   a. First supporting argument
      i. Evidence or example (include citations)
   b. Second supporting point
      i. Evidence or example (include citations)
      ii. Evidence or example (include citations)

After the completion of the literature review outline, a student will have enough literature collected and organized (sufficient detail to allow readers to follow the logic and sequence of main ideas along with citations) to construct a proper problem statement and begin writing an effective first chapter of the dissertation. At this point, formal completion of Chapter 2 follows completion of Chapter 1 (this book chapter is organized to help students in this order).

Writing the First Dissertation Chapter: The Introduction

The first chapter in the dissertation is the Introduction and is written to inform readers about the topic researched, its significance, and how the research will be conducted. A literature overview is included, where the students write summaries to show what is already recognized about the proposed research issues and to demonstrate the cognizance of a dissertation student on the topic. The precise configuration of this chapter will vary depending on university expectations and students' organization of the sections. Typically, a standard qualitative dissertation Introduction includes the Problem Statement, Purpose Statement, Research Questions, Theoretical Framework, Definitions, Limitations, Delimitations, Ethical Issues, and a Summary. Longer sections can be divided into subsections, which can be further divided if needed. The introduction of a phenomenological dissertation should introduce the study in such a way that it simultaneously provides details of the study and an overview of the study's conclusions. Students will usually begin the introduction with a statement related to the human or social problem they are discussing in their phenomenological study.

Before writing the formal problem statement, students may want to begin with a short introductory paragraph or a few paragraphs to introduce their chapter. While starting with a "hook" to get a reader interested in a writer's topic is often encouraged in writing standard papers, it is not required in research papers. With that said, it can enhance the introduction and is certainly acceptable. Students may want to write something that engages readers with provocative quotes, disconcerting statistics or interesting stories. If a more straightforward approach is warranted or desired, students can simply state the problem explicitly, beginning their introductory paragraphs with declarations like, "I will illuminate" or "I seek to understand." Following that, students should write a paragraph that gives readers an idea of the structure of the rest of the document. For example,

In this chapter, I will discuss relevant literature that relates directly to my study about the lived experiences of teachers working with student who have experienced trauma. I will then explain the method of this research, followed last by . . .

Example of an Opening to Chapter 1

Christian men spend more time exploring their understanding of masculinity than other men (Singleton, 2004), and self-help literature for Christians is usually written by evangelical Christians (Donovan, 1998; Singleton). Evangelicals quite often have a different understanding

of psychological problems than the rest of the population so the implications of healing from sexual addiction can be quite different for evangelical Christian men when compared to others. Many evangelical people believe that psychological problems are the product of a "sinful and spiritually fallen condition" (Kwee, Dominguez, & Ferrell, 2007, p. 4). Many evangelical insights are discussed in self-help literature that is targeted for evangelicals, but research about evangelical belief systems is limited in general scholarly literature. Hence, counselors who do not work with evangelicals or are not aware of evangelical belief systems are limited in their abilities to work effectively with this population. This qualitative investigation is specific to evangelical Christian men who classify themselves as sexually addicted and is aimed at focusing on these men's lived experiences of sexual addiction through their evangelical perspectives. This research will provide counselors with an enhanced understanding of evangelical Christian men who struggle with sexual addiction issues so that they can work with them more effectively.

After this, the problem statement will follow under a new heading.

Problem Statement
• •

Phenomena are not problems by definition, so writing a *problem* statement is not always in line with phenomenological research. For example, the phenomenon of discrimination may be a problem, but the phenomenon of prayer is not, at least in the social sciences. While in most cases, phenomenological studies are not aimed at solving problems at all, they can still be a phenomenological problem. Discrimination and prayer would be problematic in the sense that they need to be explained. What is the essence of prayer? What is the essence of discrimination? Those are the problems of phenomenological inquiry. While phenomenological methods are used to illuminate phenomena and reveal complexities of different experiences, they also often *create* problems to solve.

Regardless of the problem statement debate in phenomenological inquiry, students still need to write section that helps the dissertation committee understand that the proposed phenomenological research will fill a meaningful gap in current literature for the field. If a university allows, the "Statement of the Problem" can be omitted, or rather, renamed to something more suitable like "Significance of Research." Since many colleges and universities devise specific dissertation requirements that obligate students to follow a necessary structure that includes clear headings such as Problem Statement, Purpose Statement, and Research Questions, and so forth, many students must state a problem statement regardless of the proposed methodology. For ease and clarity, this chapter is written using universal dissertation headings to help students write their phenomenological dissertations within the most common dissertation configuration. Students are encouraged to deviate from this heading structure as their universities allow.

Typically, the problem statement is the center of the dissertation, and this will be the place that most committee members will read first to identify and assess the importance of the proposed research. The problem statement is also one of the most difficult portions of the dissertation to get right. From reading a problem statement, a reader should know what the problem is, why it needs fixing, and how that's significant to the field of study. Then students should propose how their research will solve that problem. After reading the problem statement, committee members should know why a student is doing a study and be convinced of its importance. It is clear how the research fills a meaningful gap that is absent in the literature.

Students often misinterpret the requested "gap" they need to produce in literature to mean that the topic presented is simply missing or limited in current research and bears further study, thereby supporting their proposal to study it. While a "gap" in current research literature is certainly missing or limited in information, that missing or limited information is not necessarily a problem. For example, in the counseling field, one may not know how much wood a woodchuck would chuck if a woodchuck could chuck wood. This is clearly missing in counseling literature. However, students need to ask themselves if this is a problem for counselors! Probably not. So while there is a technical "gap" in woodchuck-chucking behavior in counseling literature, it is not a "meaningful gap." Counselors do not need to know this information to enhance the counseling field, and a counseling student might have significant difficulty proposing this topic as a problem statement.

Problem statements should also be succinct yet thorough. Students need not elaborate on every study in the problem statement.

Save that type of writing for the literature review. Problem statements can stay within the length of one to two paragraphs. Briefly write what is relevant to highlight the problem. With that said, dissertation writers should still explain everything to their readers without assuming their readers automatically know what they, the writers, mean. Just because a problem is noted does not mean that the reader knows the solution for the proposed field of study. Students need to do this all for their readers. Be succinct and thorough. Below are five points that students should present in their problem statements.

1. State the dominant problem.

2. State the population that is affected by this problem.

3. State the type of phenomenological study (transcendental, hermeneutic, or hermeneutic with a supporting theory).

4. State what type of data will be gathered (lived experiences).

5. State how understanding the lived experiences of said population will help resolve the problem.

Here is an example of how a student might write the fifth point, which is often the most difficult:

Because interviews provide deeper insights into the intricate interactions of this population's experiences, this phenomenological investigation is best suited to exploring and identifying the specific issues of women who work in male-dominated work settings. Understanding the lived experiences of women who work in male-dominated work settings can assist in helping career counselors create stronger therapeutic alliances by offering a clearer understanding of this population's individual experiences through narrative. By illuminating specific issues of women who work in male-dominated work settings that are separate from other work settings, this phenomenological study could also help add rich information for future creation of career development tools.

In reviewing the final problem statement for quality, students should be able to respond affirmatively to the following questions in the following box:

How to Create a Quality Problem Statement

1. Do I present the research problem succinctly and thoroughly?

2. Do I present the problem in a way that responds to previous research studies?

3. Do I provide evidence that the problem is currently relevant to the field or discipline of study?

Purpose Statement

The aim of a purpose statement is a concise statement that connects the problem being addressed with the focus of the study. The purpose statement is made up of three major components: (1) the motivation driving the dissertation; (2) the significance of the research; and (3) the research questions addressed. Students must not forget to include that the intended research is phenomenological (and what kind, hermeneutic or transcendental, for example). Below is an example of all three components included in a concise paragraph:

The purpose of this hermeneutic qualitative phenomenological study is to illuminate the experiences of male counselors who work with women who experience trauma. By interviewing male counselors at trauma centers throughout Alabama, I will describe the phenomenon of the male counselor's experience of working with traumatized female clients. As a result of this study, counselor educators can better explain how their male students might experience female clients' traumas, potentially highlighting the topics of building resiliency and implementation of self-care. The question, "What are the lived experiences of male counselors who work with female clients who have experienced trauma?" is the focus of this research study.

In reviewing the final purpose statement for quality, students should be able to respond affirmatively to the following questions in the following box:

1. Do I begin my statement concisely ("The purpose of this study is . . .")?

2. Do I state that this study is qualitative, phenomenological, and the specific type of phenomenology?

3. Do I state the central phenomenon to be explored?

4. Do I use qualitative terms such as *illuminate, explore, describe, discover,* or *understand*?

5. Do I describe the participants in the study?

6. Do I note where the study will take place or from where the data will be collected?

Research Questions

Phenomenological research questions have one unwavering rule. The inquiry must always be about experience as lived. Phenomenological inquiry is only about experience and nothing else. To ask people's views about something is not phenomenological. For example, "How do teenage girls describe friendship in high school?" is not a phenomenological question since opinions and descriptions are the focus. A phenomenological question could be created by changing the focus to experience: "What are the lived experiences of friendship among teenage girls?" Students can also add sub-questions to focus more on specifics, but they are not always necessary. A sub-question might be, "How do teenage girls experience friendships in relation to social pressures?"

Research questions must not assume that something is present. Above, it was stated that teenage girls experience social pressures. Was this an assumption? No, because the phenomenon of social pressures among teenage girls has been proven throughout literature. However, if there is no connection made in the literature between the population studied and a certain phenomenon, it should not be assumed in a research question. For example, when dissertation students ask the research question, "How do teenage girls experience friendship amid homework stress?" they assume that all teenage girls are stressed about homework. That may not necessarily be the case. If the case of homework stress among teenage girls has not been studied and proven in literature, dissertation students should not assume it exists. However, if homework stress is the focus of the dissertation in relation to friendship, then it cannot be omitted, of course. Hence, the two words, "if any" often rectify the research question easily. For example: "How do teenage girls experience friendship amid homework stress, if any?" In this way, all necessary components are included in the research question without leaping to an assumption.

In each research question, students should succinctly describe what they want to understand. All major components of that population should be included. For example, if students want to ask about the marital experiences of male veterans struggling with PTSD, five components must be included among the research questions: experience, male, veteran, PTSD, and marriage. The most basic phenomenological question is phrased simply, "What are the lived experiences of such and such population?" Flow is also important, however, and "What are the lived experiences" format may not always work best. In this example case, a student might ask, "What are the lived experiences of marriage in male veterans who are diagnosed with PTSD?" but that sounds a bit awkward. A student can begin there and then reorganize. One suggestion might be, "How do male veterans who are diagnosed with PTSD experience married life?"

How to Create Quality Research Questions

- Do all the research questions ask about experience?
- Are the research questions free of assumptions?
- Are all the components of the study included in the research questions?
- Are the research questions easy to understand with no need for clarification?

Theoretical Framework

Theoretical frameworks exist in research because, to increase objectivity, a researcher must take others' thoughts into consideration. By looking at phenomena through different perspectives, researchers are able to broaden their understanding of those phenomena. In phenomenological research, the framework is phenomenological philosophy. A better heading would be Grounding Philosophy or Philosophical Framework, if renaming general headings is allowed by the committee. Phenomenology is the essence of something as it is described and how the essence of something is described in terms of how it functions in the lived experience and how it shows itself in consciousness as an object of reflection.

The two main theoretical frameworks that dissertation students can use to frame their phenomenological studies are the philosophies of Edmund Husserl (for transcendental or descriptive phenomenological dissertations) and of Martin Heidegger (for hermeneutic or interpretive phenomenological dissertations). These are the foundational philosophers. Students can use additional frameworks to frame their phenomenological studies (like feminist theory or developmental theory, for example), but only with hermeneutic studies (i.e., Heidegger). However, if students choose to use a secondary theory as a lens in their hermeneutic phenomenological study, the research would be a hybrid and should be titled that way. Students utilizing developmental theory would have a developmental-hermeneutic phenomenological study, for example.

While phenomenological researchers can use various phenomenological philosophers to frame their studies, Husserl and Heidegger are foundational and will always be included. Since most dissertation students are novice researchers who are new to phenomenological philosophy, it is best to choose either Husserl or Heidegger as the main philosophers and keep it straightforward. To identify the best philosophy for their dissertations, students will need to decide how they comprehend understanding. Husserl and Heidegger differed on this matter, and created two very different phenomenological philosophies. Below is a short summary of each philosopher's approach.

Edmund Husserl

Edmund Husserl (1859–1938) is considered the father of phenomenology. He believed that phenomenology was presuppositional. This means that, when using transcendental phenomenology, there can be no use of theoretical frameworks. His philosophy does not allow for that. Husserl believed that nothing should be assumed or taken for granted when trying to understand a phenomenon.

Husserl wanted to get to the pure essence of a phenomenon, of the way one looks at something. **Intentionality** is the fundamental property of consciousness, of looking at something. It is our awareness of something. This is the principal theme within his philosophy. **Reduction** is also a term that Husserl uses. It is basically the intentional consciousness of using the process of **bracketing (epoché)**, or, as it was once aptly called, phenomenological vigilance (van Kaam 1966, p. 259). What that means within reduction is suspending your judgments to focus on the studied phenomenon. It is not about eliminating biases but suspending them or setting them aside. **Noesis** means to thinking about, and **noema** is the thing that is thought about so those two go hand in hand. The horizon is the present experience that you are having right now. Right now, you are reading this book, that is, the experience you are having in the present, the **horizon.** This present experience that you are having cannot be suspended or bracketed because you are currently in it. Everything has a horizon when we look at any phenomenon—there is always this present experience. Therefore, nothing can be fully seen in its entirety unless you were omniscient (all-knowing) which of course, no human is. So, when we look at something, even though we suspend our judgments to try to get this pure essence of something, we come to the horizon, and the horizon is the understanding that we have.

Husserl applied to research

Bracketing is having this position so that the researcher becomes like a stranger in a strange land—kind of like an alien coming down to planet Earth for the first time. So the biases that this alien has are already suspended because the suspension is putting oneself into a position of being a stranger in a strange land. What if I didn't understand what trauma is? What if I didn't understand what rural area is? This state of being a stranger in a strange land is bracketing. In this state of intentional suspension, one can get to the essence of something. So one can see how using another theoretical framework is impossible in Husserl's philosophy. If you are suspending all other understanding in the process of bracketing, you would have to suspend any additional frameworks too. You couldn't get to the essence of something with an additional framework.

Husserl believed that all human thinking was linked to something, which simply means that when people think, they always prescribe an ending point to their thinking. Essentially, all thinking, for Husserl, was thinking something. Husserl also believed that everything we know has an objective existence, independent of ourselves, but when we discover it or know about it, that act of knowing makes that thing subjective as well because we name it, essentially. In other words, when we name something, the name becomes an obstacle between us and the object (or the things themselves). Husserl believed that it was impossible to use any kind of thinking and knowing that was not linked to language to really understand something in its essence. His fundamental premise of **intentionality** stated that the very act of thinking bonds us to the thing we think about. So, to minimize the problem of having the subjective thought overwhelm the objective existence of something as we aim to know it, Husserl proposed that individuals need to position themselves differently in the world and how they think about things.

People think when they analyze, categorize, generalize, and discriminate between things (Willis, 2001), and there are other times when people's minds are really struck by certain ideas, being moved by them. In the latter case, people are receptacles of ideas that incite in them certain feelings. The former ways of thinking are more proactive ways of thinking about something. Both exist within human thinking. Husserl believed that the more people thought about their thinking, the more they could know something clearly. They could then move from naming experiences to ordering them into more general categories within their language and how they see the world (Willis, 2001).

Key terms to include in the framework

1. **Bracketing/Epoché**—suspending judgments to focus on analysis of experience

2. **Horizon**—present experience, which cannot be bracketed; therefore nothing is fully seen in its entirety as none of us are omniscient

3. **Intentionality**—fundamental property of consciousness and principal theme of phenomenology; our awareness in a sense

4. **Noema**—what is thought about

5. **Noesis**—thinking about or interpreting

6. **Phenomenological reduction**—intentional consciousness using process of bracketing or epoché (suspending judgments to focus on analysis of experience)

Martin Heidegger

Martin Heidegger (1889–1976) branched off from Husserl and created his own philosophy (hermeneutic). He believed that there was no way we could bracket our experiences because we are always in the world with others in the circumstances of existence. There is no way to separate yourself from being within the world, and this state, this being in the world meaning *Dasein*, literally being there. *Dasein* is what Heidegger talks about when he talks about the self. Myself, yourself, each person is *Dasein*, in the circumstances of each one's own existence. If bracketing is not allowed, how can you get to the essence? If we cannot suspend our judgments to get to the essence of a phenomenon, can it really be understood? Heidegger's solution to this was the **hermeneutic circle**. He talked about it as a revisionary process. Heidegger called preconceived knowledge **fore-sight** or **fore-conception**. As we begin to understand and interpret something, our fore-sights (biases or understandings or judgments) are revised. The hermeneutic circle is a description of the process of understanding. It is not a technique that you use. This is the philosophy—What is understanding and interpretation? This is what Heidegger's philosophy encompassed—how people make sense of the world. However, in data analysis, the philosophy of the hermeneutic circle is used in this way:

When you analyze data, there is an understanding of the whole (the entire transcript) and analyzing the whole as you read it, and then there is an understanding of parts (codes and themes).

As you are analyzing data, you break down information into parts and then synthesize, and you look at the whole again (the entire transcript). That is the new understanding. And then as you move through it again in analysis, the parts make sense of the whole and the whole makes sense of the parts, and this hermeneutic circle continues until a new understanding emerges. Analysis is not a linear process; it is circular, or a better explanation is that it is *spiral* since *circular* would mean that one's understanding does not really change since a circle gets back to the same point. In a *spiral* process, understanding increases by moving from the understanding of parts to the understanding of the whole and again back to parts, continually changing as new data are introduced.

This is how Heidegger understood interpretation. This is how people make sense of a phenomenon in the world. He believed that interpretation is a constant revision. As I am interpreting something, I have a pre-understanding of the phenomenon, and as I get new information, there is a revision of that understanding. As a researcher, I grasp the whole text in individual parts and also as a whole again and again in a circle until there is a full understanding of the phenomenon. As I look at little pieces, I get these "aha" moments in relation to the whole. So you can sort of think of something you have experienced in your life and you might understand parts of it, and in 3 years you have new experiences, and you can think back on past moments, and they are understood in new ways as you have learned new things throughout experience. This is how the whole has an impact on the individual parts and how the individual parts have an impact on the whole. There is always a moving from the object that is to be understood to the personal comprehensions of the researcher and then back to the object (Heidegger, 1971).

Heidegger applied to research

Heidegger's framework can be seen as the use of lenses. In the technique of using the hermeneutic circle, you want to make your personal biases or judgments explicit, either by writing them in your dissertation or journaling about them somewhere before you analyze data. As you write before the process, why did you understand something some way? For example, if someone uses a term, you might know exactly what they mean because you "get" that context. In Hawaii, there are many common terms used. If a participant said, "We are ohana," you might understand that to clearly mean "we are family" in a specific way because you understand Hawaiian culture, either because you live there or in other ways. Husserl would go back to the participants and ask, "What did you exactly mean by this?" because he would not take that for granted. He is a stranger in a strange land, but in Heidegger's framework, one may have some pre-understanding and can incorporate it as appropriate. Being in a certain gender, race, experience is incorporated into data analysis. So with Heidegger, a researcher would make personal biases explicit; however, in bracketing, it is unnecessary because all personal understandings are irrelevant. Why bring them up if the goal is to suspend them? Some may argue that one needs to put biases in front of consciousness so that one knows what biases to suspend, and there is certainly an argument that can be made for that. However, biases are bountiful, and some may be subconscious. To journal about every personal bias about a phenomenon is unrealistic, maybe impossible. Hence, journaling would typically not accord with bracketing, but it would with the hermeneutic circle.

Gadamer took Heidegger's concept of the hermeneutic circle and further developed it, so if you are doing this research, get his book, as it's essential to understanding the hermeneutic circle in depth. The lenses discussed in the Heideggerian framework above are **pre-understandings**; Gadamer calls them **fore-conceptions**. A person modifies the nature of understanding by this constant process of renewed projection (interpretation). This happens through each lens. By looking through one's biases and understandings (instead of trying to suspend them), researchers revise understanding. So researchers are always looking through these changing lenses (new understandings) in order to understand a phenomenon. Each lens is created as the process of interpretation continues. So one can see how this allows for another theoretical framework. If a researcher is using attachment theory, for example, pre-understanding would be one lens, attachment theory would be another lens, and a new understanding would emerge from each lens.

Key terms to include in the framework

1. *Dasein*—"being there"

2. **Fore-sight/fore-conception**—preconceived knowledge about a phenomenon

3. **Hermeneutic circle**—interpretation as revision, it is a description of the process of understanding and not a technique

How to Create a Quality Theoretical Framework

- Is the main philosopher introduced with all key terms?

- Are connections among key terms of the framework logical and applicable to the research?

- Does a secondary theoretical framework follow (only in hermeneutic phenomenology) in terms of how it will be used as a lens?

- If using a secondary framework, is there a final summary of how both frameworks will work together?

Definitions

In this section, students should provide succinct definitions of the primary concepts discussed in their dissertations. Terms that may have multiple meanings should be defined as well. Definitions that do not need to be included would be common terms or terms that can easily be looked up. Students should include citations for each definition.

Assumptions

In hermeneutic phenomenological dissertations, it is particularly important to discuss assumptions or biases about the research topic. In hermeneutic phenomenology, the understanding is that biases cannot be set aside or bracketed, and therefore, they need to be recognized and later revised as new information is discovered. If doing a hermeneutic study, students should elucidate aspects of the study that are assumed but cannot be established as fact. Only assumptions that are essential to the meaningfulness of the study should be described and why those assumptions are necessary to illuminate in the context of the study. In transcendental phenomenological dissertations, biases are irrelevant. They are set aside and should not be made explicit. Highlighting biases in a transcendental phenomenological study is counterintuitive to the process. Students may want to note this in an Assumptions section if it is required by the university. They can discuss the process of bracketing a bit more here to demonstrate how assumptions will be handled and why it is essential not to highlight them.

Delimitations and Limitations

Delimitations are different from limitations, and it can be confusing to delineate the two. In summary, delimitations are choices made by the researcher which should be mentioned. They describe the boundaries that you have set for the study. This is the place to indicate the things that you are not doing and explain why you have chosen not to do them. Limitations are methodological weaknesses. They are influences that are out of the researcher's control. Any **limitations** that might influence the results should be mentioned. Common limitations for phenomenological dissertation studies are small sample sizes, time limitations, and bias in the participant sample. Note that the Limitations section should be relatively brief and straightforward, simply mentioning major concerns and reasonable measures to address those concerns.

Significance

In describing the significance of a study, students should discuss how their research would benefit or have an impact on others. In essence, readers should be able to understand how individuals or groups of individuals could benefit from the proposed research. Students should identify how the study would advance knowledge in the field of study and, if applicable, how the study could contribute to or have an impact on certain practices or policies in the field of study. Potential implications for positive social change can also be discussed here as long as they are restricted to the scope of the study. Students should use the problem statement to guide them in identifying the significance of their study. They should also write from general to specific, like the funnel system in writing a literature review. Begin with the general contribution of the study (How does this study contribute to society?) and continue to narrow the focus toward the field of study and research question (How does this study contribute to understanding of PTSD among teenagers?). This type of writing enables readers to understand the problem and solution generally and then more specifically in a logical way.

Summary Sections

The Summary section should not be too long but should have purpose. Students should summarize the main points of each chapter and provide a transition to the next chapter. This portion of the chapter is a succinct paragraph.

Completing the Literature Review

Once the Introduction is finished, students will finish writing the Literature Review. If all steps were followed, a good part of the literature review was started along with a preliminary outline, which can be expanded as necessary. Students should be careful not to write a literature review that has little to do with their research questions. This type of disorganized writing is avoided by following the literature review outline initially created in the literature review strategy. In a well-written literature review, a reader reads the research question or questions toward the end as a natural progression from what was stated above. A proper order, from general to specific, will allow the reader to think in a deductive way and stay focused on the research topic.

Another important strategy for creating a quality literature review is how journal articles and other relevant literature are presented from each section of the outline. Dissertation students should not write literature reviews by writing a series of article critiques one after another. This kind of writing will destroy the flow of the manuscript. Ideally, the literature review should begin with the problem statement as the introductory paragraph followed by studies that support the introductory paragraph in more detail. Similar studies should be discussed together, with an emphasis on more relevant studies. For example, if a dissertation topic is about the lived experience of stress on teachers in rural areas, the literature review should be written in a way that would present teaching stress literature as a group and rural area literature as a group. Throughout the process of appropriately grouping similar articles, students should also present similar research findings together. If a few studies on teaching stress have the same finding, students should state the finding and then cite all the studies with that finding. Only studies that are similar to the dissertation topic should be described in great detail. Using sub-headings is also beneficial for organizing a literature review and should be used when appropriate.

Lastly, literature reviews should be balanced. Relevant research needs to be presented in terms of strengths and weaknesses along with alternate studies that present differing results. All studies should be synthesized in a way that they are relevant to the dissertation research questions.

How to Create a Quality Literature Review

- Are studies related to the research topic and phenomenological method presented from general to specific?

- Is the literature review organized by topics rather than by author or date?

- Are similar studies grouped together with major studies discussed in detail and minor studies with more restriction?

- Is relevant research compared and contrasted, nonconclusive results noted, and described in terms of its strengths and weakness along with alternate studies? Can readers draw their own conclusions?

- Can readers summarize what is known as well as what is not known about the research topic in the related discipline?

- Are studies reviewed and synthesized as they relate to the research questions?

- Are most articles current (within 5 to 10 years) and recent developments in the problem emphasized?

- Does the literature review provide a complete explanation of the problem and how the dissertation study will fill a meaningful gap in the literature?

- Are all necessary citations provided for statements of fact with no assumptions or leaps in logic from the author?

Literature review exercise

Below is a portion of a literature review example uploaded from University of West Florida's website (Literature Review: Conducting & Writing) with some of my editing for easier reading and clarity. Overall, the student did a nice job of covering the information needed to support her research question about communication in the family after a family member is diagnosed with a chronic illness. Notice the funnel effect from general to more specific and ending at the proposed research question, how the student mentioned some studies in more detail than others, and how the narrative flowed from one thought to the next instead of listing one study after another. There are many ways that this literature can be improved as well. It might be helpful to look at the table above on how to create a quality literature review and check where the student was successful and what areas needed improvement. You can also check the student's original literature review online or in Appendix E to see where I edited the literature review for flow and grammar (something that is beyond the scope of this book but still important to learn).

Literature Review

Chronic physical illness and chronic mental illnesses are reviewed separately in this literature review due to the tremendous differences in the two. In this study, they will be compared against one another to cross-analyze the differences and similarities in how the family member is treated depending upon his or her type of illness.

Chronic Physical Illness

Chronic physical illnesses vary in types and intensity but have one characteristic in common: They recur throughout time, usually at random intervals. The uncertainty that comes along with a diagnosis along these lines can greatly affect family communication and relationships.

Marriage. Marriage is the basis of most families in many cultures. Keeping the marital bond strong could be very difficult in the face of a chronic physical illness. A chronic physical illness could potentially change the daily lives and interactions of the entire marital relationship. It is important to discuss the communication that occurs around theses illnesses in order to understand how those who have one have been treated since their diagnosis based on research already conducted around similar communication processes. Couples that used relationship talk or talking about the nature and direction of the relationship, chronically ill couples had more benefit than a couple that did not include someone who had a chronic physical illness did (Badr & Acitelli, 2005). This literature proves that in a situation where a spouse is chronically ill, it is important to use communication to make one another aware of certain things such as how one felt about a situation, or what one needs or expects from his or her partners. Talking about the state of the relationship can be helpful for chronically ill people to express fears in relation to their illness and the marriage. Collaborative talk is the type of communication that is commonly correlated with positive results (Berg & Upchurch, 2007). This shows that it is important for married couples to talk about their situation together to keep their relationship strong since these tactics have been proven to be helpful for the couple. Couples that are aware of their partner's expectations of communication in the marriage are more successful in supporting one another (Shuff & Sims, 2013). Being aware of the partner's desires and being able to fill them is central to satisfaction in the relationships' functioning. Marital coping and sharing are not limited to relationship talk though. Another powerful way of sharing within the family is through narrative.

Narratives. Something that is strongly recognized and praised throughout literature on chronic physical illnesses is narratives. Several studies (Freeman & Couchonnal, 2006; Ott Anderson & Geist Martin, 2003; Walker & Dickson, 2004) stress the importance of narratives for the family healing process. Narratives are beneficial because they allow research to capture personal accounts of illness, and let the ill person be a gatekeeper to his or her own information about the illness. Ott Anderson and Geist Martin (2003) state that those with a chronic physical illness are more likely to actively share if their feelings and perceptions are confirmed by other people, especially friends and family. Some chronic illnesses have a negative social stigma to them, and confirmation that people will be respectful is important to getting the patient to open up about their experiences. Narratives and storytelling help families to communicate about changes that have taken place. Ott Anderson and Geist Martin (2003) conclude that the ever changing identity in the face of illness never stops, it is an endless development.

Sharing through narrative in cases of chronic physical illness has the potential to better family communication because the patient is able to clearly and concisely explain what is happening to him or her from their personal point of view. This can help the family identify what the patient has gone through, as well as understand new emerging identities. However, Lorde (1980) points out an important paradox where sometimes patients may be empowered by giving a narrative account of their story, while others may feel anxiety from reliving those moments of their life. When participants used communication to reduce their fear of their illness, they were likely to communicate about their illness more often (according to Grotcher & Edwards, 1990). Narratives are important in understanding and meeting the expectations of the family members when they are chronically ill (Walker & Dickson, 2004). Often, people will have expectations for their family members without verbally expressing them, leaving family members more often than not confused about what direction to take. However, a narrative or forms of storytelling in the case of a chronic physical illness may reflect some of the patients unfulfilled needs and help family members to identify them.

Chronic Mental Illness

A chronic mental illness can be extremely hard for families to cope with given the negative social stigmas that exist about the illness in most societies around the world today. A chronic mental illness in a family member could lead to almost constant care and monitoring, depending upon the illness and the intensity. Families may find it difficult to cope with or come to terms with a family member's diagnosis of a chronic mental illness due to the many challenges it presents. Much of the literature surrounding mental illness in the family is psychology based, and there is a strong need for communication-based studies to better understand these unique families.

Marriage. An important aspect of the family dynamic is marriage. It is the foundation of most families and gives people feelings of stability. Communication is essential to marriage, but little literature exists exploring the communication around a diagnosis of a mental illness. However, much literature exists on its effects on marriage. Perry (2014) focused on social networks and stigma in relation to those with a serious mental illness. A spouse is a very prominent and strong part of a married person's social network. If someone is entering or exiting a marriage, his or her social network changes in different ways. Perry (2014) found that the stigma of a mental illness had contact with the social network and the relationship between the two works ambiguously together. Meaning that the social network responded to the mental illness through their own thinking and proving that spouses typically control family conversations. Spouses decide the climate of the family views and values toward different topics as they raise their offspring, if they choose to have any. There is a strong call for communication scholars to explore the way that families interact, especially about mental illness, and that a positive or a negative attitude can set a precedent for what future family communication will be like based off of how spouses interact (Segrin, 2006). The different communication processes that couples partake in set examples for how children interact.

Wives who are depressed are more likely to make an aggressive comment to their husbands than wives who are not depressed would, and depressed wives have less positive discussions than their counterparts (Schmaling & Jacobson, 1990). These aggressive statements could likely become a stressor for the marriage or produce a negative schemata of marriage for children or adolescents in the family. Depression has a large impact on the family, and usually just creates more problems that tends to result in fueling depression (Segrin, 2006). However, this assertion could also be true of the communication patterns surrounding may other types of mental illnesses in the family.

Parent–Child. Looking at the parent–child relationship in reference to mental illnesses, it is known that parents are the primary caregivers to children and adolescents with chronic mental illnesses. Literature mainly focuses on the illness from the parents' perspective, rather than the child's, suggesting that little is known about children's perceptions of their parents' mental illnesses. Parent's feelings of loss about an adult child with a mental illness focuses on grieving about ambiguous losses, like the child's loss of self or identity (Richardson, Cobham, McDermott, & Murray, 2013). This loss and grieving process has the potential to shape the families' behaviors and patterns of communications. Since there are usually no tangible effects of a mental illness, parents may often find it hard to cope with a diagnosis and come to terms with it. Even harder for families to process is the fact that in most cultures and societies in the world, there is a negative social stigma to having a mental illness. Parental grief over a child's mental illness is not socially acceptable (Richardson et al., 2013), and several studies noted that parents felt as though they needed to hide their child's illness or their grief about that illness (Chadda, 2014; Richardson et al., 2013). Most of the struggles that parents in this situation face are with the topics of self-concepts and identities, with variance to whether it is their own, or their child's. Richardson et al. (2013) found that the child's illness changed the parents own identity. Since the identity and self are such fluid concepts, it is important to understand the self and different identities as well as the changes that occur with the two in accordance to both the parents and the children. There is little literature about mental health's effects on self-concepts and identities.

Hamond and Schrodt (2012) explored the effects of the different parenting styles on children's mental health and concluded that there was no statistically significant evidence that the different styles had an effect on mental health. However, acts of affection and authority make limited, but important, improvements to the child's mental health (Hamond & Schrodt, 2012). When it is the parent in the relationship who is mentally ill, the communication process is entirely different. When adolescents internalize and externalize behaviors were correlated to parents' mental illness, parents with mental illnesses were found to have a negative effect on the adolescent or child, the whole family, and even the parent and child's interactions (Van Loon, Van de Ven, Van Doesum, Witteman, & Hosman, 2014). This literature exemplifies that parental mental illness controls more channels of communication than a child or adolescent's mental illness does. While much literature exists about families and mental illness, unfortunately very few scholars focus on the talk that occurs about the family member with the illness and the communication around this topic.

Reviewing the literature leads back to the question: How are those with a chronic illness treated by their families since their diagnosis? Analyzing both mental and physical illnesses and the family communication processes around them are essential to furthering the conversation that communication scholars are creating to understand these unique families.

While the literature review example above is not perfect (Whose dissertation is perfect? After all, this is typically the first attempt at research by a student.), it is a suitable example to illustrate how to discuss topics in a funnel effect so that the discussion ends at the research question. Students should use headings to delineate different topics from more general to most specific. If an outline was created prior to writing the literature review, creating headings should be fairly straightforward.

REFERENCES AND
SUGGESTED READING

Finlay, L. (2009). Debating phenomenological research methods. *Phenomenology & Practice, 3*(1), 6–25.

Gadamer, H. (2004). *Truth and method.* New York, NY: Continuum.

Heidegger, M. (1962). *Being and time* (J. Macquarrie & E. Robinson, Trans). Oxford, England: Basil Blackwell.

Heidegger, M. (1968). *What is called thinking?* (J. Glennray, Trans.). New York, NY: Harper & Row.

Heidegger, M. (1971). *Poetry, language, thought* (A. Hofstadter, Trans.). New York, NY: Harper & Row.

Heidegger, M. (1982). *The basic problems of phenomenology.* (A. Hofstadter, Trans.). Bloomington: Indiana University.

Howell, K. E. (2013). *An introduction to the philosophy of methodology.* Thousand Oaks, CA: Sage.

Husserl, E. (1931). *Ideas: General introduction to pure phenomenology.* London, England: George Allen & Unwin.

Husserl, E. (1962). *Ideas: General introduction to pure phenomenology.* (W. Boyce Simpson, Trans.). New York, NY: Collier.

Husserl, E. (1964). Introduction to transcendental phenomenology (Introductory essay). In P. Koestenbaum (Ed.), *The Paris lectures.* The Hague, Netherlands: Martinus Nijhoff.

Husserl, E. (1973). *Experience and judgment: Investigations in a genealogy of logic.* (L. Langrebe, Ed.). London, England: Routledge & Kegan Paul.

Little, M. K. (n.d.). *Living with chronic illnesses: How are those with a chronic illness treated by their families since their diagnosis?* Retrieved from https://libguides.uwf.edu/c.php?g=215199&p=1420828

Pan, M. L. (2017). *Preparing literature reviews: Qualitative and quantitative Approaches* (5th ed.) London, England: Routledge.

Smith, D. W., & McIntyre, R. (1984). *Husserl and intentionality: A study of mind, meaning, and language.* Boston, MA: D. Reidel.

van Kaam, A. (1966). *Existential foundations of psychology.* New York, NY: Image Books.

Willis, P. (2001). The "things themselves" in phenomenology. *Indo-Pacific Journal of Phenomenology, 1*(1), 1–12.

Wrathall, M. (2006). *How to read Heidegger.* New York, NY: W. W. Norton.

References in Examples

Donovan, B. (1998). Political consequences of private authority: Promise Keepers and the transformation of hegemonic masculinity. *Theory and Society, 27,* 817–843.

Kwee, A. W., Dominguez, A.W., & Ferrell, D. (2007). Sexual addiction and Christian college men: Conceptual, assessment, and treatment challenges. *Journal of Psychology and Christianity, 26*(1), 3–13.

Singleton, A. (2004). Good advice for Godly men: Oppressed men in Christian men's self-help literature. *Journal of Gender Studies, 13*(2), 153–164.

Literature Review Example

Badr, H., & Acitelli, L. K. (2005). Dyadic adjustment in chronic illness: Does relationship talk matter? *Journal of Family Psychology. 19*(3), 465–469. doi:10.1037/0893-3200.19.3.465

Berg, C. A., & Upchurch, R. (2007). A developmental-contextual model of couples coping with chronic illness across the adult life span. *Psychological Bulletin, 133*(6), 920–954.

Chadda, R. K. (2014). Caring for the family caregivers of persons with mental illness. *Indian Journal of Psychiatry, 56*(3), 221–227. doi:10.4103/0019-5545.140616

Freeman, E. M., & Couchonnal, G. (2006). Narratives and culturally based approaches in practices with families. *The Journal of Contemporary Social Services, 43*(3), 198–208.

Grotcher, J. M., & Edwards, R. (1990). Coping strategies of cancer patients: Actual communication and imagined interactions. *Health Communication, 2,* 255–266.

Hamond, J. D., & Schrodt, P. (2012). Do parental styles moderate the association between family conformity orientation and young adults' mental well-being? *The Journal of Family Communication, 12,* 151–166. doi:10.1080/15267431.2011.561149

Keyton, J. (2011). *Communication research: Asking questions, finding answers.* New York, NY: McGraw Hill.

Lorde, A. (1980). *The cancer journals.* San Francisco, CA: Sheba.

Ott Anderson, J., & Geist Martin, P. (2003). Narratives and healing: Exploring one family's stories of cancer survivorship. *Health Communication, 15*(2), 133–143.

Perry, B. L. (2013). Symptoms, stigma, or secondary social disruption: three mechanisms of network dynamics in severe mental illness. *Journal of Social and Personal Relationships, 31*(1), 32–53. doi:10.1177/0265407513484632

Richardson, M., Cobham, V., McDermott, B., & Murray, J. (2013). Youth mental illness and the family: Parents' loss and grief. *Journal of Child and Family Studies, 22,* 719–736. doi:10.1007/s10826-012-9625-x

Rosland, A. M. (2009). *Sharing the care: the role of family in chronic illness.* Oakland, CA: California Health Care Foundation. Retrieved from https://www.chcf.org/publication/sharing-the-care-the-role-of-family-in-chronic-illness/

Schmaling, K. B., & Jacobson, N. S. (1990). Marital interaction and depression. *Journal of Abnormal Psychology, 99,* 229–236.

Segrin, C. (2006). Family interactions and well-being: integrative perspectives. *The Journal of Family Communication, 6*(1), 3–21.

Shuff, J., & Sims, J. D. (2013). Communication perceptions related to life-threatening illness in a relationship: A Q methodology study. *Florida Communication Journal, 41*(2), 81–96.

Van Loon, L. M. A., Van de Ven, M. O. M., Van Doesum, K. T. M., Witteman, C. L. M., & Hosman, C. M. H. (2014). The relation between parental mental illness and adolescent mental health: The role of family factors. *Journal of Child and Family Studies, 23,* 1201–1214. doi:10.1007/s10826-013-9781-7

Walker, K. L., & Dickson, F. C. (2004). An exploration of illness-related narratives in marriage: The identification of illness-identity scripts. *Journal of Social and Personal Relationships, 21*(4), 527–544. doi:10.1177/0265407504044846

Ward, B. W., Schiller, J. S., & Goodman, R. A. (2014). Multiple chronic conditions among U.S. adults: A 2012 update. *Preventing Chronic Disease, 11,* E62.

Methodology

In Chapter 3 of the dissertation, students will present the plan for research as well as provide philosophical grounding. Students need to present a solid presentation of their understanding of the phenomenological tradition being used (transcendental or hermeneutic) and why the chosen phenomenological method is best for answering the research questions. The purpose of phenomenological research is to generate the lifeworld experiences of a certain population. Even though there is no fixed set of methods to conduct phenomenological research, there are methodological guidelines to follow and expand upon. A study is written well when readers can replicate it by reading the methodology.

Introduction

Just like all chapters of their dissertations, students will begin the third chapter with a brief introduction. Students will briefly restate the purpose of the study along with a short summary of Chapter 3. This is written straightforwardly as follows: *In Chapter 3, I present the research methods design and rationale and my role as the researcher. I discuss the selection of participants and instrumentation along with research procedures. In addition, I explain . . .*

Design and Rationale

In this section, students should restate their research questions exactly as they wrote them in Chapter 1 of the dissertation. Central concepts of the study should be presented and defined along with the research tradition, which is phenomenology. Rationale should be provided for the phenomenological study. Students should discuss why phenomenological method is most appropriate for the chosen topic. One effective way to do this is to compare and contrast phenomenological method to other methodologies. For example,

For this study, I aim to use phenomenological methodology because it allows me to illuminate rich descriptions and personal meanings of lived experiences related to [insert topic here]. While the method of ethnography is used to identify shared patterns of a cultural group, it is not appropriate for my study since culture is not the focus of this research. A case study approach, which allows the development of detailed portrayal and case analysis of a single case or numerous cases, was considered but did not fully meet the requirements of focusing only on experiences as lived.

Essentially, this section is for students to summarize the phenomenological methodology that will be used and give reasons for why it is a good strategy for the study. Students will typically include the following:

1. The specific research methodology that will be used (transcendental phenomenology or hermeneutic phenomenology)

2. Background information about either transcendental phenomenology or hermeneutic phenomenology, which would include how it is defined and applied

3. The intended outcome for using phenomenology (focus is on illuminating lived experiences and only lived experiences)

4. The suitability of the chosen phenomenological method for the study (this would be a good place to compare and contrast other methods)

Researcher Role

In this section, students will need to explain their roles as observers and as participants in their phenomenological research studies. If there are any personal or professional relationships with participants, they should be noted here. Perhaps a researcher works with some participants at a hospital or previously supervised participants, for example. The aim is to disclose any relationships and to assure that any positions of power are avoided between researcher and participants. How personal biases are addressed need to be included in this section as well as any other ethical issues and a plan to address those issues. If a student is working on a transcendental phenomenological study, the process of bracketing will be addressed here. In hermeneutic phenomenological studies, students will discuss the hermeneutic circle. These explanations should be general and succinct.

Participants

Dissertation students need to describe the population of interest, providing demographic information about the population to be sampled. Information can include age range, gender, job title, ethnicity, and geographical location, for instance. In short, anything that is relevant to the study in terms of demographics should be noted. For example, if a student is writing a dissertation about the lived experiences of teenagers working with support animals, she might want to include participants' ages, genders, support need, and the type of animals. Students will also need to discuss how they will sample participants. Purposeful sampling and snowball sampling are great to use together since students may receive referrals from participants about other potentially interested participants. While the sample size is certainly something to consider, saturation (reaching a point where no more new data are being obtained from participants) is the key focus in qualitative work and should be noted as the goal rather than including an estimated sample size. To summarize, students will include the following elements in this section:

1. Participants—Include demographic information such as age range, gender, job title, ethnicity, geographical location.

2. Sampling—Usually purposive, criterion, or snowball sampling (or a combination) is advised.

3. Sample size—Students can state a range of participants needed for the study (typically between 8–15 depending on the text referenced), the rationale for that number, and need to, most importantly, describe the relationship between saturation and sample size and that saturation is the goal rather than a number of participants.

4. Criteria—List specific criteria for participants to be able to participate in the study.

5. Recruitment—Explain detailed procedures for how participants will be identified and how they will be contacted and recruited. Perhaps a flyer will be posted in classrooms or an e-mail will be sent to a listserv that has subscribers who fit the research study demographic. If a flyer is used, students should attach the flyer in the appendices of the dissertation.

Instrumentation

In phenomenological research, instrumentation typically includes some combination of interviews, follow-up interviews (to address any gaps in data like misunderstandings, missing information, unclear information, etc.), focus groups, field notes, journaling, audio recording, and video recording. A combination of instruments is ideal rather than one so that findings are rich, but dissertation students should also be realistic about choosing various instruments so that they do not overwhelm themselves with unrealistic expectations. When students present their research instruments, they should be specific about the strengths and weaknesses of each type of instrument to be used and need to discuss how the chosen instruments are sufficient to answer the research questions. Here is an example using interviews and follow-up interviews as instruments:

Follow-Up Interviews

It was expected that many of the descriptions provided in the initial individual interviews will need further extrapolation. Forgetfulness, limited or inferior vocabularies, and limitations in subjects' fully expressing themselves all contribute to subjects' deficient explanations (Kruger, 1988, p. 152). Follow-up individual interviews allow me to clarify the preliminary information gathered or gather additional data that may not have been expressed in the initial interview. After my first reflection on the data, something relevant is often discovered where further clarification is needed, and the clarifications are obtained through follow-up interviews. The data are then further analyzed until the meaning is completely clear (Giorgi, 1985).

Procedures

In this section, students need to discuss the "what, when, where, and how" of the study. What will be done? When will each step happen? Where will each step happen? How will each step happen? It is important to note that this section should be written so that another researcher could read the procedures and replicate the study. An introductory paragraph is appropriate to begin this section before another heading is introduced. Here is one example:

This research highlights important elements of this phenomenon as it is lived and how it is experienced. This focus on how something is experienced informs the lived aspects of human phenomenon. Descriptions of lived experiences are essential in order to avoid methods of investigation that are indirect (Giorgi, 1985).

Data Collection

This section will detail each data-collection instrument and how it will be utilized. In most cases, this will include interview protocols or focus groups along with either field notes, journaling, or both. Important points to include the following:

1. From where will data be collected?

2. Who will collect the data?

3. How often and how much will data be collected? (focus is on saturation here)

4. How long will it take to collect data?

5. How will data be recorded? (ex: transcriptions, video recordings, audio recordings)

6. What are the follow-up procedures? (these might be follow-up interviews)

Follow-up plan of recruitment results in too few participants. Below is an example of how to write this section in a step-by-step fashion so that it can be replicated by the reader.

A semistructured interview is used for the initial individual interviews to permit the essential methodical spontaneity of phenomenological research (Giorgi, 1985). Individual follow-up interviews are used to fill gaps that exist in the data collected. Gaps consist of either excluded data or areas that are implicit or deficient in any way (perhaps the participant did not finish a narrative for one reason or another) (Giorgi, 1985). This method of collecting data first allows the lived essence of circumstances to operate spontaneously through the first interview and then are assessed more precisely (Giorgi, 1985). The preliminary individual interviews, the follow-up interviews, and the observations of the researcher are the key methods of collecting data in this study.

Every participant is notified of possible threats and potential benefits of research participation and provides written consent for participating in the study. Confidentiality is protected by giving each participant a code (ex: P1, P2, P3, P4, P6, P7, and P8). Codes are used in analyzing data, and I am the only person who knows the identities of the participants.

Interview Questions

When constructing an interview protocol for a phenomenological study, students can choose a structured, unstructured, or a semistructured interview process. Structured interviews allow researchers to choose specific questions that cover a range of topics specific to the research question(s) but limit the ability to deviate from specific content, which does not allow sufficient opportunities for the research participants to share unanticipated information that is relevant to the research topic. Unstructured interviews allow for plenty of deviation from the chosen interview questions but students run the risk of failing to address all the elements relevant to their research topic if participants digress to other topics. A semistructured interview protocol is recommended, allowing students to construct interview questions relevant to the research question so that key aspects of the research study are sure to be covered while allowing for participants to discuss other information that may end up being relevant to the study. Semistructured interviews allow students to keep a balance between focusing on the research topic and allowing for a disciplined naturalness in phenomenological research (Giorgi, 1985).

When constructing interview questions, students must only ask about experiences and not about thoughts, feelings, or perceptions, for example, "When did you first feel like you had a best friend? What happened?" When interviewing participants about their lived experiences, participants may often provide opinions and descriptions as answers because they are the cognitive tools they have to describe those experiences. However, those answers would not be relevant because experiences are different from thoughts and are analyzed differently. For example, did you ever have an opinion about someone or some situation and later discovered you were wrong when you thought or felt about it more or talked to someone else about it who gave you a different perspective or as you moved forward in life and had different experiences that changed your mind? This is why thoughts and opinions are not relevant or reliable at getting at the essence of a phenomena. Just because a participant thinks something happened a certain way may not be the case when the experience is discussed. Researchers would ask participants to talk about an experience when they had a certain opinion to try to uncover the essence of that phenomenon. For instance, "You stated that you were unfairly treated by your employer. Can you discuss an experience in your life when you felt unfairly treated like that?" The participant may say, "I was late a few times at work, and he just flipped out and fired me. I mean, it was ridiculous!" The experience may not indicate that the employer was unfair at all.

When interviewing participants, students can give participants a brief introduction about the focal point of the research to set the tone and then ask participants to describe their lived experiences as if to someone who had never heard of the phenomenon being studied. In the example below, the phenomenon being studied is sexual addiction and religiosity. Yes or no questions are fine to use to avoid assumptions about experiences or to clarify, but most questions should be open ended (and, of course, about experiences).

Interview guide

1. *Describe the nature of your sexual addiction.*

2. *Has your religion had an impact on your sexual addiction?*

3. *If not, discuss how your religion has remained separate from your sexual addiction.*

4. *If so, give an example of a time where your religion had an impact on your sexual addiction.*

5. *Has your religion had an impact on your views about sexuality in general?*

6. *If not, give examples of how your religion remained separate from your views about sexuality.*

7. *If so, give an example of a time where your religion had a helpful impact on your views about sexuality.*

8. *If so, give an example of a time where your religion had a harmful impact on your views about sexuality.*

Follow-Up Questions

After the initial interviews, students should transcribe and review the written transcription. Whether students transcribe their own interviews or hire someone to do it for them is simply a decision of preference. However, it is important to note that transcribing an interview and listening to participants' voices during transcription can be an important part of the process of analysis. After all, many things may not be noted while merely reading a transcript when the spoken word is omitted. Certain inflections, tones, accentuation, tempo, acceleration, modulation, and things that may go "unsaid" are all part of the data. It is very difficult to determine what percentage of communication is nonverbal in nature. A big part of communication is also *how* things are said rather than *what* is said. One estimate is that "no more than 30 to 35 percent of the social meaning of a conversation or an interaction is carried by the words" (Birdwhistell, 2010), meaning that 65% to 70% of communication is conveyed through nonverbal cues. In that regard, I encourage students to transcribe their own interviews, but if time is an issue and the service is hired out, listening to the recording along with reading the transcript is recommended. Students can take notations on the transcript if they hear certain things in spoken word that are not reflected in written word (tones of anger, sarcasm, etc.). After reading the initial transcript, students will find that, in many cases, there is incomplete, unstated, misunderstood, missing data or any areas that seemed unfinished or implicit. This is where follow-up interviews are employed to fill in these gaps in information. Students will construct follow-up for each participant solely based on the gaps in the descriptions given. Those follow-up interview questions should be written down and used for each follow-up interview.

The data collection method of using semistructured interviews and follow-up interviews allows the lived sense of participants' situations to function spontaneously in the initial interview with more detailed assessment of descriptions utilized later. Students need to also remember that the phenomenological study is about illuminating experiences, and this delineation is important to remember during interviews. Often, participants will discuss viewpoints about something rather than experiences. Viewpoints are not the focus of a phenomenological study. If participants discuss views rather than experiences, students can easily redirect the participant by asking, "Can you give me an example of when you have experienced this?" For example,

Participant: I think my mom resented me because she blamed me for my father leaving.

Researcher: Can you give me an example of an experience you had when you felt this resentment or blaming?

Participant: Let me think, yes, okay, one day when I was about 10 years old, I overheard my mom on the telephone talking to one of her friends. She was complaining about how difficult it was to be a single mom, and she said that if she didn't have us kids to raise that our dad would never have left. She said something specific about me too. She said that I was the most challenging of all of us kids and that it's hard to control her temper around me. I agree with that. She would yell at me more than at my siblings, and when I grew up and we would argue, she would say, "If it wasn't for you, your dad would never have left."

Students are encouraged to change their interview questions as appropriate. As participants are interviewed, new interview questions will surface, and others will change for upcoming interviews. Students should note how their interview process has developed throughout the study in their journals or in other notes and include this information in their Results chapter.

Focus Groups

Focus groups are also an option for collecting data and offer some distinctive benefits over individual interviews as well as place some limitations. In groups, people behave differently than individually or with only one other person (in this case, the researcher). Focus group interviews can challenge participants to reconsider or intensify personal views. Confrontation happens in groups and is mostly absent in individual interviews. Participants can feel validated or conflicted by others depending on what is said in the group. The dynamics are very interesting in focus groups, and completely different kinds of data can emerge. Focus groups can also be used in combination with individual interviews, perhaps meeting with a focus group to discuss a certain topic and then meeting with each participant individually to build on the information discussed in group. If a research topic is considered sensitive or traumatic, focus groups are actually beneficial data-collection methods because many people are more willing to share their sensitive experiences within a group and feel more supported among people who share similar experiences that are typically difficult to discuss. Confidentiality and ethical considerations are always part of the decision-making process on whether to use groups or individual interviews, and students should discuss any ethical considerations with using focus groups with their committee members.

Journaling

The decision to journal in phenomenological research may or may not be suitable depending on the type of phenomenological study that is chosen. If a student is completing a hermeneutic phenomenological study, using Heidegger's philosophy, personal biases need to be made explicit. Journaling would be a good way to do this. Students could write down any of their biases, their pre-understandings about a phenomenon prior to analyzing data. In this way, they could deliberately put their biases in front of them, fully expecting that they could be revised as data are analyzed. They could journal as they analyzed data in order to keep track of the revisions in their thinking about a phenomenon.

In transcendental phenomenological studies, using Husserl's philosophy, bracketing is necessary. Hence, all personal understandings are irrelevant. The researcher is approaching the data as if he or she is a stranger in a strange land. Biases are suspended by not taking anything for granted. There is no reason to journal and place biases in the forefront since they are unconnected to the phenomenon being studied. Journaling is not necessary when approaching bracketing or epoché in this way. However, some students may choose to journal about their biases in order to know what to suspend. This is, of course, an option. However, people have so many personal biases, and many emerge as they experience new things and have conversations, and as researchers as they analyze data. To journal about every personal bias about a phenomenon prior to data analysis so as to know what to bracket is unrealistic. Hence, I contend that journaling does not typically correspond with the process of bracketing. However, transcendental phenomenology requires that researchers think about their thinking in an effort to position themselves in a way that they are not dependent on their subjective minds. Journaling would be a very good exercise for reflecting upon one's thinking in an effort to see the phenomenon more objectively. The more transcendental phenomenological researchers think about how they think, the more they can think proactively and contemplatively about a phenomenon. More about journaling strategies using either method of phenomenology is discussed further in the data analysis section.

Data Analysis

The term *data analysis* is not completely in line with phenomenological inquiry simply because *analysis* means to "break into parts," whereas phenomenological inquiry seeks to understand a phenomenon as a *whole*. In transcendental phenomenology, the goal is to illuminate the essence of a phenomenon, the entirety of it, without the corruption of personal bias. In hermeneutic phenomenology and the use of the hermeneutic circle, the parts inform the whole and the whole informs the parts. If something is broken into parts alone, the phenomenon is lost as a whole. Hence, other terms are more appropriate in phenomenological research. *Explication* is one such term, which means an "investigation of the constituents of a phenomenon while keeping the context of the whole" (Hycner, 1999, p. 161). Of course, not all dissertation students may have the ability to change headings depending on their universities' dissertation standards, so the decision to change "data analysis" to "explication" is posed as an option and certainly not a requirement. For the purposes of clarity and uniformity, "data analysis" will be used throughout this book.

Since the goal of phenomenological research is to illuminate the lived experience of a phenomenon, the method of analyzing data is emergent. What this means is that data emerge and change during analysis. In a narrative, a lot of characteristics make up the story: characters, social interactions, cultures, objects, time references, beliefs, and more. If any of those characteristics changed within a narrative without changing the fundamental meaning of that narrative, then those characteristics would not be essential themes in a phenomenological data analysis. For example, in a narrative about "the lived experience of urban farming" vital themes could include matters of working in city and city-adjacent areas, using creative spaces (like rooftops for gardens and the use of national parks), working within restrictions on raising animals (chickens vs. rabbits), and zoning issues. One could not replace *urban farming* with *rural farming* and keep the essence or meaning of "the lived experience of urban farming." The themes would change completely. Hence, the goal of phenomenological data analysis is to present a description from essential themes of an experience in a way that is comprehensible and identifiable to anyone who has had that particular experience. It should be apparent how one experience of a phenomenon differs from other experiences that are similar.

When analyzing phenomenological data, students should immerse themselves in the descriptive world in an empathic way. They need to live through their participants' descriptions as if they were their own. Students need to slow down and dwell on each narrative, not passing over any details of the account as if they understood them but dwelling on the details of each situation that is described. Each description should be magnified and amplified; even what may seem like a minute explanation for the participant needs to be of great importance to the student researcher. In summary, phenomenological data analysis is the process of transcending the mundane nature of each description to reveal the essence of the phenomenon.

General steps for phenomenological data analysis are provided below to give students a foundation to write a thorough data analysis section capable of being replicated. When using these steps, students need to also highlight transcendental or hermeneutic explanations in their analysis to demonstrate their use of their chosen phenomenological method. Suggestions for delineating chosen phenomenological methods follow the data analysis steps. A flowchart is also recommended and pictured below.

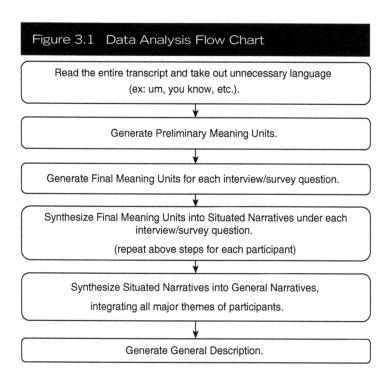

Figure 3.1 Data Analysis Flow Chart

Read the entire transcript and take out unnecessary language
(ex: um, you know, etc.).

↓

Generate Preliminary Meaning Units.

↓

Generate Final Meaning Units for each interview/survey question.

↓

Synthesize Final Meaning Units into Situated Narratives under each
interview/survey question.

(repeat above steps for each participant)

↓

Synthesize Situated Narratives into General Narratives,
integrating all major themes of participants.

↓

Generate General Description.

General Data Analysis Steps

Step 1: Reading and deleting irrelevant information

The initial step in data analysis is to read the individual interview transcript in its entirety to discern the participant's complete story. This step also consists of deleting any information that is irrelevant or unnecessary, like repetitive statements or filler linguistics like "um," "uh," "well," or "you know."

Example of Step 1

ORIGINAL TRANCRIPTION:

Student: "So, I actually have um this my regular full-time job and I also have . . . Well, now I have two other jobs as well. So, the um, my, my ability to engage with the program as much as I'd like is limited. That's . . ."

Interviewer: "Okay."

Student: ". . . I do, I do engage with bits. So, because we have the reporting requirements in terms of the, I think it's minimum of three per week as well as the two assignments per week."

REVISION:

Student: "I actually have my regular full-time job, and I also have two other jobs as well. So my ability to engage with the program as much as I'd like is limited. I do engage with bits because we have the reporting requirements in terms of its minimum of three per week as well as the two assignments per week."

Step 2: Preliminary meaning units

The second step in this method is to create preliminary "meaning units" (Giorgi, 1985, p. 10) while concentrating on the research topic. A meaning unit is the allocation piece of data that reveals a feature or trait of the phenomenon being investigated.

Example of Step 2

The first meaning unit describes F3's view of his or her role as a facilitator, and the second meaning unit is viewing his or her role as one who stimulates discussions.
"My role as (1) facilitator is to (2) provide prompts."

Step 3: Final meaning units

Next, I broke down all the preliminary meaning units to final meaning units (or themes), which were informed by my deepened understanding of each participant's description.

Example: Step 3

Question 6:   Please describe how students are interacting and connecting with each other in the classroom.
        F3
Preliminary meaning unit 1: Students share similar experiences among culturally similar students to support each other.

Preliminary meaning unit 2: Students support each other professionally and personally.

Final meaning unit: Students support each other.

Step 4: Situated narratives

This situated narrative was a reiteration of each participant's story where I organized specifics and experiences thematically under the specific interview or survey questions. The meanings of each participant's experience were highlighted thematically through direct quotes from the interviews and surveys.

Example: Step 4

Remind Students of Assignments Due
F1

"Let's say the discussion ends on Sunday; I remind them Monday, Tuesday, Wednesday that is [an] individual project and if they have problems. So just reassuring that they are aware of the submission day."

F4

"If we're coming toward the end of the week, I check if there are important requirements that students should have fulfilled. And if not, then I usually put out an announcement. I put out an announcement at least once a week, and toward the end of the week."

F5

"Then at the end of it, for instance, they now have to do summaries, so I try to make sure I guide them timewise on everything. One instance, you know, 1 or 2 days before the summary, or this is what you should be looking at. It's almost time to submit. Are you getting your groups together?"

Step 5: General narratives

I created general narratives from the situated narratives, unifying participants' accounts into a general description of all the participant's narratives. The goal was to organize the data from the situated narratives while highlighting all of the participants' meanings of their experiences.

Each narrative was organized by the interview or survey questions.

"Most" = saturated theme

"Many" = 50% theme

"Some" = theme that was unsaturated but relevant when unity was not established on a certain question

Example: Step 5

Q1: What do you consider to be your role and responsibilities in the classroom as a student?

Most students thought their primary role was to be a learner and considered their responsibilities in the classroom to be attendance and participation, being prepared with required readings, and engaging in the discussion forums. Many also added that they were responsible for completing course assignments, learning from other students, and being respectful to others online.

Q6: When teachers talk about "critical thinking" or "higher order thinking," what does this mean to you?

Most students differed on their thoughts about what critical thinking meant. Many thought that providing references to back an argument and critical analysis were both indicative of critical thinking. Some thought that application and synthesis were elements of critical thinking.

Step 6: General description

The final step of the analysis was the general description, which moved away from the participants' everyday perspectives. The aim was to discuss the themes that were implicit in all or most of the participants' descriptions of their experiences ("Some" was used at times when needed to address a topic where participants varied in responses). The aim was to unite the major phenomenological themes into a cohesive general description.

Example: Step 6

During a typical week in the online classroom, faculty check their messages and address student concerns. They read students discussions in the discussion forums and post their own responses to students, and they grade students' submissions. Many faculty post a summary of each week's discussion or a wrap-up announcement of the week's lesson at the end of the week for students. Most faculty also post reminders for students about due dates and spend their time providing students with extra resources in the classroom.

Delineating Transcendental Phenomenology in Data Analysis Steps

In transcendental phenomenology, the process of bracketing through phenomenological reduction needs to be highlighted in the data analysis steps. This can be done by writing something about your process of journaling to bracket, inserting a step between Steps 2 and 3, or a combination of both options.

Journaling

If students choose to use journaling to bracket their biases, they may journal about their role as students and the experiences they had with their faculty facilitating a discussion. After noting their experience, they will then separate their experience by examining it and exploring it in terms of varying experiences other students have with the same phenomenon. Then, they either confirm their suspended experience as authentic to the phenomenon studied or remove it from their analysis as biased information. The goal is to note a bias and then suspend it in an effort to look at it from various alternative angles so that students can verify it as true to the essence of the phenomenon or a belief to exclude. Students need to think about the way they are thinking about the phenomenon in order to be less dependent on their subjective mind and to see the phenomenon for what it is, the thing itself. This thinking about thinking is often termed *metacognition* and students can search for different activities on metacognition to help them create a journal suitable for transcendental phenomenological work. Activities like concept mapping and metacognition note-taking skills are two great activities (Vancouver Island University, 2018).

Follow-up interviews

The researcher must be preoccupied by the concrete to understand and explain the essence of a phenomenon. To demonstrate this concept, consider the game of chess. Chess can be described as a game, a sport, a gift, an heirloom, among other descriptions, depending on the context. By discussing chess as a sport, a context of competition and risk may come to mind. The word game, on the other hand, may change the meaning of chess altogether, despite the synonymous grammatical understanding of both (Giorgi, 1985). Since subtle nuances in descriptions have the potential to alter meanings, the interpretation of participants' descriptions into meaning units, which is a practice that requires shifts in terminology, must be performed with great attention to detail.

In reflecting on and then interpreting the narrative, researchers must consider the context of the situation in order to carefully choose wording to express the meaning unit. Often, they will need to modify a vernacular that is used in narrative into more understandable dialect. They should consistently confront language as if they were strangers in a strange land and not depend on preconceptions as a way to understand the phenomenon. Students need to note each meaning unit literally and within the discussed context, as it is stated by each participant in terms of the research question. Then they will compare and contrast meaning units. Combine meaning units that are similar into final meaning units. If a concrete interpretation cannot be obtained (for example, a participant may use colloquialisms or slang to explain concepts), researchers will follow up with the participant for clarification in a follow-up interview rather than assuming they know what the participant meant. (What did you mean when you said, "After the discussion started really rolling, I was just riding the wave of excitement with the other students.") This would be an extra step inserted into the general data analysis between Steps 2 and 3:

After Step 2, I had to collect additional data through individual follow-up interviews. After I discovered any gaps in the data (such as omitted information or confusing statements) in the transcript of each initial individual interview, I prepared additional interview questions for each participant to fill in those gaps. I interviewed each participant for further explanation of each identified gap. I then transcribed the individual interview, read it, and integrated it into the original analysis of meaning units.

Delineating Hermeneutic Phenomenology in Data Analysis Steps

In hermeneutic phenomenology, there is a focus on the interaction between the researcher and the data. Each participant's experiences are translated through the researcher by comparison and contrast of accounts with the accounts of other participants discussing their experiences of the same phenomenon. This is, of course, done through the hermeneutic circle by modifying the nature of understanding by a constant process of renewed understandings of the phenomenon. In the data analysis steps, students using hermeneutic phenomenology need to illustrate their use of the hermeneutic circle. This can be done by writing something about your process of journaling and follow-up interviews as a way to record and revise your experiences, assumptions, and interpretations about the phenomenon studied.

Journaling

The researcher must make personal biases explicit, anticipating projections in the quest for understanding, and this can be most easily done through journaling. Hermeneutic phenomenological researchers discuss how they use journaling to concentrate on the data during ceaseless distractions and biases that are continually created within. They want to note that the goal is always to replace their current conceptions with more fitting ones through reflection (Gadamer, 1975, p. 269). Through journaling, they necessitate the revision of personal biases, as those personal biases create the questions necessary for thought revision (the hermeneutic circle). Every revision of a preconception has the ability to develop a new projection of meaning. Contending projections can arise alongside one another until an agreement of meaning is clarified (Gadamer, 1975).

Follow-up interviews

In hermeneutic phenomenological analysis, follow-up interviews are often needed to clarify researcher preconceptions so they should be incorporated in the data analysis steps (between Steps 2 and 3). Interpret meaning of what is stated by each participant within the context of the situation with an openness to revisions of current understandings. The context of a situation is crucial in interpreting phenomena; it guides researcher in staying faithful to "the things themselves" (Heidegger, 1927, p. 153) but can sometimes be misunderstood due to personal biases or understandings. Ask questions through your biases and current understandings to capture each participant's authentic meaning. An example of what this might look like is illustrated below:

A research participant discussed his frustration over his recent poor academic performance. Because I, the researcher, knew that the participant had parents who demanded high academic performance, my preconception was that the participant felt frustrated due to his strict upbringing and that he would disappoint his parents. This preconception directed my clarification question. After the follow-up interview, a clarification was made, and my new projection of meaning was that the participant felt guilty because of his helplessness to fix the problem on his own without the help of a tutor.

Participant: I would often think, "I can do this. I can solve this on my own. I can do better and get my grades up. I had to, but I couldn't. It was so frustrating!"

I: Did you feel frustrated because you thought you would disappoint your parents?

S6: No, it was because I felt like a failure, and I knew that I couldn't do it on my own.

Using Software

Qualitative data analysis software is used to organize data through coding so that researchers can illuminate themes about a phenomenon. Although qualitative data analysis software can make some qualitative data analysis easier, phenomenological studies do not fall in this category. There are significant concerns among researchers about using data analysis software for completing quality phenomenological analyses. Some phenomenologists state that the process of coding is unwarranted because the goal of reading transcripts is to familiarize oneself with the transcript. When using qualitative data analysis software, researchers can view transcripts as *data* rather than dwelling on what was said in the interview texts to ascertain the essence of the phenomenon being studied. Qualitative data analysis software can limit a researcher's ability to dwell on a text because it essentially separates the researcher from the data (Goble, Austin, Larsen, Kreitzer, & Brintnell, 2012), hinders abductive reasoning (van Manen, 2014), and instrumentalizes a process that should be intuitive (Cross, 2011).

I encourage students to hand code their phenomenological dissertations because the using software in a phenomenological dissertation requires more work than coding by hand if a quality phenomenological dissertation is the goal. However, it can be done, and it is worth the discussion here so that students know what is involved in qualitative data analysis software use.

How a researcher uses qualitative data analysis software makes all the difference in producing a quality phenomenological research study. Brian Kelleher Sohn (2017) is one such researcher who advocates the use of qualitative data analysis software when appropriate and shows how to use qualitative data analysis software within the phenomenological tradition. Here are some things students may need to discuss in their phenomenological dissertations to support their use of qualitative data analysis software. Many of these steps can also be used to enrich manual coding of phenomenological data:

1. When coding or memoing, consistently remember that the words being read were uttered by a human being who lives in a certain context in the world with others.

2. Analyze data with a goal of staying immersed in the information and the entire experience rather than using it to cut data down to smaller, more manageable parts.

3. Keep memos to help track personal reactions to the data being analyzed. These memos will help bring you back to a point where a certain part of the data created a personal revelation or provided you with a certain frame of reference.

4. Listen to the participants' voices from the video or audio recordings so that you can sense their experiences on a deeper level and stay immersed in the experience of what is being stated. This process supports abductive thinking in phenomenological analysis. Do this anytime you are feeling distant from the participants due to reading and organizing codes.

5. Reread the entire transcript at any point when you feel distant from the stories uttered or the contexts of the participants.

6. Every few weeks during the analysis, utilize a group of other researchers or students to read the participants' transcripts (with all identifiers omitted) and discuss what stands out for them in reading participants' experiences. These sessions will serve to help you look at experiences that you may have missed through allowing software to code and organize your data and will challenge you to understand the phenomenon in terms of others' understandings. It will also validate some understandings you have about the data analyzed. If you are using bracketing, this process will help you suspend personal judgments by viewing data through the eyes of others and can broaden your horizon of understanding. If using the hermeneutic circle, this process will help to revise current understandings through others' feedback, which may differ from yours.

7. Read and reread phenomenological studies and works of relevant phenomenological philosophers and discuss them with the research group in terms of the transcripts and data analysis. This will allow you to stay within the phenomenological tradition and let the theoretical lens help you gain unique insights about the phenomenon you are studying.

8. Take breaks from data analysis to interrupt it, something van Manen (2014) terms "passive activity" (pp. 345–346). This will allow you to gain further insights into the phenomenon that you may miss with consistent immersion in the data.

9. Use the data analysis that you compiled in the software as an assistant to your final written narrative of the lived experience. Do not simply cut and paste the themes that emerged. You must vividly portray the phenomenon through experience in written word, and qualitative analysis software will limit this ability. You will need to discuss what moved you in the analysis and prioritize the findings in relation to what was illuminated for you as the researcher and in terms of what you presented in your literature review about this population and phenomenon.

Validity and Reliability

When discussing how to address threats to validity and reliability (or qualitative rigor if different terms are allowed by the university), students should be realistic about what they can reasonably accomplish in a dissertation as sole researchers. Below are eight procedures by Creswell and Poth (2017) a student may utilize to assure validity in the dissertation. Some are practical for a dissertation study, and some are not. Students should choose appropriately.

1. **Prolonged engagement and observation in the field of study**—spending extensive time with participants in their natural environments and building trust with them to gain a better perspective of their context and situation, to warrant more depth in the data analysis, and to limit misrepresentations in the data because of the presence of the researcher. Students will also explore details of the phenomenon to a depth that will allow them to establish what is important and what is irrelevant.

2. **Triangulation**—using numerous sources of information, methods of data collection, or several researchers in analysis. This could be a research team of colleagues within a field of study wherein each researcher analyzes the data with the same data-analysis protocol. The different findings would create a broader and deeper understanding of the phenomenon. Most forms of triangulation are time consuming, and it requires greater planning, organization, and resources that may not be available to dissertation students. While triangulation is one very common technique for addressing validity in a study, it may not be realistic.

3. **Peer review**—meeting with a neutral colleague who asks questions about the methods, results of the study, and any other emerging conclusions in an effort to create accountability and honesty. Modifications made due to peer interaction should be noted in the dissertation. Much of this sounds like what is routinely done with one's dissertation committee, but committee review is not always enough to establish validity and reliability.

Students should not assume that committee review is peer review with the goal of validity and reliability as a result.

4. **Negative case analysis**—Hypotheses are developed about a phenomenon after extensive fieldwork, and then instances are sought that contradict the hypotheses. If researchers do not find any conflicting situations, the hypotheses that were developed are considered reliable. If contradictions arise, the hypotheses that conflicted are modified. Negative case analysis continues until all hypotheses are modified until there are no more contradictions. This type of analysis is utilized for multiple studies of the same nature rather than solitary studies such as dissertations.

5. **Explanation of researcher bias**—revealing personal biases and preferences in journals, field notes, and data analysis protocol. Much of this process is discussed throughout this chapter, depending on the phenomenological method used. It is important to note that if a student only verifies everything that was already believed about a phenomenon at the end of the study, the method of inquiry was probably inappropriate, or bias overshadowed proper data analysis. Phenomenological studies should always end with discovery to be credible.

6. **Member checking**—Transcripts are typically reviewed by participants who provided the information for accuracy. In member checking, there is usually an expectation that participants should also review the interpretations of their experience and agree that the conclusions are credible. However, some participants may not agree with the results, and that does not mean that the results are inaccurate. Hence, I advise students to ask that their participants verify the accuracy of the transcripts but not the accuracy of the interpretations.

7. **Rich descriptions**—providing a detailed account of participants' experiences where pattern and themes are put into context. Context is key in rich descriptions, showing the complexity of the lived world of participants.

8. **External audits**—having a researcher who was not involved in the *research* process assess the data analysis procedure and the findings to determine whether the findings accurately represent the data.

Ethics

This ethics portion of the dissertation is largely aimed at institutional review board (IRB) expectations. Students should address any ethical concerns they have about recruitment plans and how to address them as well as data collection strategies and how to address any issues that arise. Perhaps participants choose to leave a study or refuse to participate at some point. There may need to be a response on how to address participants' potential adverse effects, for example. Ethical concerns related to confidentiality is important to discuss here and how confidentiality will be protected. In most cases, this is done through assigning participants codes and omitting any identifying information. Data storage is also important to discuss here, who has access to the data, and when and how they will be destroyed. The focus is always on protecting the participants, although in some cases it is important to note the researcher's protection. For example, if a student was exploring the lived experiences of a group of prisoners of a certain dynamic, a student may want to discuss boundaries set into place to protect both parties. Perhaps setting up a separate research-oriented e-mail to enable participants to initiate contact with researchers would be appropriate instead of providing a personal e-mail. Other ethical issues might be conflicts of interest, using incentives, and any power differentials that may present an ethical concern.

SUMMARY

As in each chapter summary, students should keep it brief with purpose. Discuss the main points of Chapter 3 and transition to Chapter 4. Always keep this portion of the chapter a succinct paragraph.

WRITE THE ABSTRACT _____

The proposal of the dissertation consists of the first three chapters, and if students have followed my book step by step, they are now at the end and ready to submit the proposal. After a dissertation proposal is submitted for formal review by the committee (and any other reviewers, depending on each student's university process), an oral defense follows. But before submitting these first three chapters, students need to write an abstract to introduce the document. The word count for a dissertation proposal varies by university, which means students need to find out expectations and stay within maximum word count. Typically, an abstract looks like this:

Abstract

This is the abstract, which is typed in block format with no indentation. It should be accurate and concise. Your abstract should also be written in a self-contained way so that people reading only your abstract would fully understand the content and the implications of your proposal. Write this section last when you have collected all the information in your proposal. Your abstract is a short summary of your entire proposal and is not a statement of what readers should expect to read in your proposal. Your committee members should be able to read the abstract and know what your proposal discusses. Avoid sentences like this: This dissertation proposal will . . .

Keywords: research, literature, methods, limitations

REFERENCES AND RESOURCES ___

Birdwhistell, R. L. (1990). *Kinesics and context: Essays on body motion communication*. Philadelphia: University of Pennsylvania Press. (Original work published 1970)

Creswell, J. W., & Poth, C. N. (2017). *Qualitative inquiry and research design: Choosing among five approaches*. Thousand Oaks, CA: Sage.

Cross, N. (2011). *Design thinking: Understanding how designers think and work*. Oxford, England: Berg.

Crotty, M. (1996). *Phenomenology and nursing research*. Melbourne, Australia: Churchill Livingstone.

Gadamer, H. (2004). *Truth and method*. New York, NY: Continuum.

Giorgi, A. (1985). Sketch of a psychological phenomenological method. In A. Giorgi (Ed.), *Phenomenology and psychological research* (pp. 8–22). Pittsburgh, PA: Duquesne University Press.

Goble, E., Austin, W., Larsen, D., Kreitzer, L., & Brintnell, S. (2012). Habits of mind and the split-mind effect: When computer-assisted qualitative data analysis software is used in phenomenological research. *Forum Qualitative Sozialforschung, 13*(2), 2.

Grbich, C. (2013). *Qualitative data analysis: An introduction*. Thousand Oaks, CA: Sage.

Guion, L. A., Diehl, D. C., & McDonald, D. (2011). *Triangulation: Establishing the validity of qualitative studies*. University of Florida, IFAS Extension. Retrieved from http://www.ie.ufrj.br/intranet/ie/userintranet/hpp/arquivos/texto_7_-_aulas_6_e_7.pdf

Heidegger, M. (1962). *Being and time* (J. Macquarrie & E. Robinson, Trans). Oxford, England: Basil Blackwell.

Hycner, R. H. (1999). Some guidelines for the phenomenological analysis of interview data. In A. Bryman & R. G. Burgess (Eds.), *Qualitative research 3* (pp. 143–164). London, England: Sage.

King, N., & Horrocks, C. (2010). *Interviews in qualitative research*. Thousand Oaks, CA: Sage.

Kruger, D. (1988). *An introduction to phenomenological psychology*. Pittsburgh, PA: Duquesne University Press.

Sohn, B. K. (2017). Phenomenology and qualitative data analysis software (QDAS): A careful reconciliation. *Forum Qualitative Sozialforschung, 18*(1), 14.

Vancouver Island University. (2018). *Ten metacognitive teaching strategies*. Retrieved from https://ciel.viu.ca/teaching-learningpedagogy/designing-your-course/how-learning-works/tenmetacognitive-teaching-strategies

van Manen, M. (2012). *Phenomenology of practice: Meaning-giving methods in phenomenological research and writing*. Walnut Creek, CA: Left Coast Press.

Results

A quality Results chapter in a phenomenological dissertation differs from other qualitative dissertations in that it needs to be grounded in phenomenological philosophy. In this chapter, students will learn how to report phenomenological research results, ground them in phenomenological philosophy, and incorporate research results in the Methods chapter to further demonstrate validity and reliability.

Introduction

Start the fourth chapter with a brief introduction and short summary of what is discussed in Chapter 4. This can be written in this way: In Chapter 4, I present the research findings and connect the findings of the study with [insert chosen phenomenological philosophy here]. I discuss the process of data collection and analysis. In addition, I explain . . .

Setting

In this section, students will describe where the study was completed and any personal or organizational conditions that may have influenced research participants' experiences within that setting that may have influenced research results. For example, participants could be influenced by changes in personnel at a job site, and their understanding of past experiences could be affected. How one remembers something is influenced by how one sees the world in present day.

Participant Demographics

In this section, students will describe the participants' demographic information. Some demographics may include age range, gender, job title, ethnicity, geographical location, for example. In short,

Table 4.1 Participants' Demographic Data

Participant	Age	Gender	University	Years Married	Ph.D. Year
P1	47	Male	Online	15	Second year
P2	35	Male	Traditional	3	First year
P3	31	Female	Traditional	10	Third year
P4	49	Female	Online	16	Dissertation
P5	37	Female	Online	1	Second year
P6	38	Female	Traditional	7	Dissertation
P7	32	Male	Traditional	8	First year
P8	50	Female	Online	25	Second year

anything that is relevant to the study in terms of demographics should be noted. A table is most appropriate in this section for easy reference. For example, if a student was presenting findings about the lived experiences of marriage dynamics during the dissertation process, a table might look like Table 4.1.

Data Collection

Under this heading, students will state how many participants were in the study, the location where data were collected (ex: Where were participants interviewed or where were focus groups held?), frequency of data collection (ex: How often were participants interviewed?), and duration of data collection (ex: How long were the focus groups or interviews?). Students will explain how they recorded the data (perhaps the interviews were audio recorded or video recorded). If there were any variations from the data collection plan discussed in Chapter 3 or any unusual circumstances encountered during data collection, they should be noted here. Perhaps the video recorder malfunctioned during an interview with a participant and a researcher used audio recording instead.

Findings

In this section, students will address each research question and present quotes from interview transcripts or other documents to support the findings. In phenomenological research, the question is often just one: What are the lived experiences of [insert phenomenon here]? Often, however, students include sub-questions, and so those need to be answered as well. Students will also

Table 4.2 Table of Themes						
Theme	**P1**	**P2**	**P3**	**P4**	**P5**	**P6**
Childhood Conflict	X	X	X	X	X	X
Feeling Disconnected From a Parent	X	X	X	X	X	X
Early Sexual Exploration	X	X	X	X	X	X
Creating a Hierarchy in Marriage	X	X	X	X		X
Affirmation Through Sex	X		X	X	X	X
Rationalizing Through God	X		X	X	X	X
Unrealistic Sexual Expectations	X		X	X		X
Problems in Marriage	X	X	X	X		
Spousal Blaming	X		X	X		
Confusion Over Spiritual Leadership	X	X	X			
Sexual Addiction as God's Will	X		X	X		
Lacking Help From Church		X	X			
Angry at God			X	X		

discuss their process of moving from codes to themes to a summary of the phenomenon and then present their final description of the phenomenon through the incorporation of their themes. The most consistent way to report phenomenological study results is to follow the step-by-step process of data analysis outlined in Chapter 3.

This final phenomenological summary should be written so that the experience described is understandable to any reader and can be identified by anyone who has had that particular experience. In turn, the description of the phenomenon should clearly present that experience differs from other experiences that are similar. Students should use quotations from the data to demonstrate the emergence of themes. Students will also need to discuss any discrepancies among participants and how those discrepancies were factored in data analysis.

In its most minimal form, phenomenological results consist of an explanation of meaning units, themes, and summaries. Meaning units are typically grouped together to form themes. Themes are combined to form a composite summary of the phenomenon. Quotes are then inserted to support the findings. Research participants will have their individual ways of experiencing a certain phenomenon, and it is the researcher's job to look for these common to all or most of the participants and to not cluster meaning units together where significant differences exist. Discussing unique experiences of participants is also important in reporting results to demonstrate rigor and to develop ideas about the phenomenon. An example of how to report results follows in Table 4.2.

Situated Narratives (Themes)

Childhood conflict

All participants reported conflict during their childhoods that were traumatic to them.

"When [my father] left, my mother blamed me for the divorce. Said that I was the cause because when I was born, my father loved me and not her anymore." (P4)

"My mother is on her third marriage. My father and my dad are not the same men. I didn't learn that until I was in the fifth grade that my dad wasn't necessarily my father, and that really impacted me." (P5)

"We got out of the car, and she took off. She left. There's three boys standing on the street crying. She just drove around the block or something and came back. I look back and I think, that's horrible! That is horrible! That's sick thinking. And that's just one of several things." (P6)

Feeling disconnected from a parent

All participants stated that they felt disconnected from either their mother or father, mostly fathers.

"[I tried] to please him and be what I could for him, and then when he up and left us, it was a huge void for me." (P1)

"In my senior year of high school, my mom and dad divorced, and he separated, and it became that much harder. I was older. I was busy. He was busy. He would make time for the younger siblings. It wasn't as much of an expectation for me." (P2)

"In between when my dad left and high school, there was very little contact between my dad and me. If I had never seen him again, it would have been just fine with me." (P5)

Problems in marriage

Participants experience problems early in their marriages. Problems were different and included things like conflict of personality, unwanted pregnancies, and emotional abuses.

"Had we not gotten pregnant, we probably never would've gotten married. So then I started to get angry. You know, I had prayed for a wife from God, and I started to get angry because she wasn't the ideal or what I thought I needed or should I say, that I wanted." (P1)

"Then I got married and because, like I said, my girlfriend got pregnant. Although we loved each other, we wanted to do the right thing, ultimately, I think there was some resentment there." (P3)

"As far as her self-esteem issues, if she had done some work with a counselor to address those issues instead of waiting 17 years into our marriage. For some of those things, she says she has to accept some responsibility." (P6)

Students can also use themes by writing more extensive summaries:

Childhood conflict

Participants discussed conflict with their parental relationships, particularly in the area of rejection. All subjects felt unaccepted as children by one of the parents. P1 felt that his mother blamed him for his parents' divorce because she felt that P1's father loved him more than he loved her. P2 found out that the father that raised him was not his biological father, and he experienced a feeling of emptiness followed by anger after finding this out. P2 described having "a huge hole in his heart" after getting this news. P3 felt that his opinion did not matter to his mother and that he needed to earn her love through doing chores and running errands. P4's parents constantly fought and eventually divorced, and though he knew that his mother loved him, he felt that his father only wanted custody of him out of spite for P4's mother. P5 said that he grew up in a strict Christian home with parents who were not affectionate toward one another. P5 stated that his mother would not spend any time to talk to him about issues with which he struggled. P6 felt like he was the "black sheep" in his family and that his parents treated him differently than his two brothers who were both valedictorians of their classes while P6 was seen as the underachiever of the family.

Feeling disconnected from a parent

Participants experienced an emotional disconnection from a parent starting from childhood, and most of them verbalized ongoing struggles with trying to reconnect with those absent parents throughout adolescence and into adulthood. P1 felt that he was never good enough for his father's standards, and after his father left the family, P1 felt a bigger emotional void. As his father was on his deathbed, P1 yearned to hear that his father thought he was significant and that he loved him, but his father never told him that before he died. After P2's mother and father divorced, he did not speak to his father very often as he was attending college, though his younger siblings continued to interact with his father. P2 thought that his father felt more obligated to spend a lot of time with P2's younger siblings, and therefore, P2 was not a priority because he was older than them. P2 also connected with his biological father after he found out that he was adopted to deal with the emptiness and anger he felt about his biological father leaving him. P3's father was not involved with the family in a way that was significant to P3. He described his father as irresponsible and absent, and P3 suspected that his mother eventually asked his father to leave the house. P3 never felt close to his father, and as a teenager, he did not have any contact with him and did not want any contact with his father. Eventually, P3's estranged father became a born-again Christian and pursued P3. With some difficulty, P3 and his father reconnected and formed a relationship. After the divorce,

P4 did not see is father. His mother had full custody of him, and his sister lived with his father. P4 felt a lot of resentment toward his father because of the volatile divorce, feeling that his father used him and tried to get custody of him only to make his mother look like an inadequate parent. P5 felt disconnected from his mother, feeling that she was not interested in talking to him about anything. He described her as "very proper" and seemed detached when he spoke about her. P6's mother was a strict parent, and he described her as being "harsh" when he was younger because "she had to be." P6 saw his father only on weekends because his father would work late through the week.

Early sexual exploration

Participants explored their sexuality in childhood and adolescence. P1 started masturbating to sexual images of women at age 12 or 13. P2 had multiple sexual partners as a teenager and was promiscuous in college. P3 first had sex with a girl he was dating in college. He later engaged in casual sex with strangers in college. P4 started . . .

General Narrative

All of the participants had family conflict that they experienced like emotional abuse and other traumas of various degrees. They experienced disconnectedness with either their mothers or fathers, mostly fathers. It was due to counseling and support groups that participants were able to realize they their parental disconnections made an impact on their unfavorable sexual behaviors as adults. While they were sexually acting out, participants felt inadequate, and most of them used sex as a way to feel better and affirm their masculinity. All of the participants sexually explored at as they grew up in childhood and adolescence, yet none of them discussed sexuality with their parents. Throughout their childhood and adolescent sexual explorations, participants felt guilt and shame because they thought it was sinful. Some of the participants . . .

General Description

The evangelical male who identifies himself as a sexual addict comprehends sexuality within a strict view of Christianity, and this Christian view conflicts with sexual exploration in childhood and adolescence. In order to cope with the opposition of Christian views and sexual desires, evangelical men split their life-worlds into different parts of *their lives. While one life-world urges them to explore sexually, another life-world follows a strict Christian sexual moral code that does not coincide. Sexual urges often overwhelm these men, and shame and guilt follow when sexual desires are acted upon. While their sexual pleasure from sexual acts give them emotional relief, they still feel conflict and guilt that follows illicit sexual acts. While the pattern of moving from sexual deviancy to pleasing God continues, evangelical men split their sexual acts from what they believe religiously, creating a sub-conscious life-world split. They often use their religious beliefs as rationalization to continue in sexual acts. Perhaps God failed them, or perhaps God will always forgive their sins after acting out sexually. Getting married is usually considered a deliverance from these men's sexual struggles, something that will end the sexual deviance. When marriage inevitably fails in this endeavor, it also generates more problems for these men because the sexual behavior continues outside of the marriage. Another life-world separation invades, the marriage space, which is separate from the spiritual space and the sexual space already created prior.*

Connecting to the Theoretical Framework

While general instructions and examples were provided above to illustrate how to present findings, a student's dissertation findings are not complete without an explanation of how a chosen theoretical framework (transcendental phenomenology or hermeneutic phenomenology) was applied. Students can connect their findings to their chosen phenomenological philosophy in many different ways.

How to Discuss the Researcher's Process When Using a Transcendental Theoretical Framework

1. **Bracketing/Epoché/Phenomenological Reduction—** Discuss how judgments were suspended to focus on analysis of experience. How did you suspend your judgments to focus on the analysis of participants' experiences?

2. **Horizon**—During data analysis, what was your present experience, your horizon? The horizon cannot be

bracketed, so you will need to discuss that not everything could have been realized by you, the researcher. This discussion might also lead into a discussion about future research implications in Chapter 5.

3. **Intentionality**—Discuss your level of scrutiny of the data you analyzed. How did you keep your focus on the topic you were studying? Perhaps you slowed down and dwelled on each narrative and did not pass over the details of the account as if you understood it already.

How to Analyze Participants' Experiences When Using a Transcendental Theoretical Framework

1. **Horizon**—What different horizons did you see throughout participants' experiences? During a participant's explanation of a present experience, what might you not have been able to see because of their current situatedness? Was there a realization later about certain ideas or understandings?

2. **Intentionality**—Identify examples of participants' intentionality. Intentionality is a participant's consciousness of something that is directed by his or her horizon of what something means or how something is perceived at that time.

How to Discuss the Researcher's Process When Using a Hermeneutic Theoretical Framework

1. *Dasein*—How has your *Dasein* affected the research? How did the research affect your *Dasein*, your being there?

2. **Fore-Sight/Fore-Conception**—What was your preconceived knowledge about the phenomenon you were studying?

3. **Hermeneutic Circle**—How were your understandings revised as you analyzed the data?

How to Analyze Participants' Experiences When Using a Hermeneutic Theoretical Framework

1. *Dasein*—How was participants' "being-in-the-world" with others? How did participants find themselves in situations that were not of their making? How did participants actualize their *Dasein* or fail to actualize?

2. **Fore-Sight/Fore-Conception**—What was participants' preconceived knowledge about certain experiences or situations and how did this knowledge change?

3. **Hermeneutic Circle**—How did participants revise their interpretations or understandings about different situations in their experiences?

Validity and Reliability

Students will discuss how they implemented the strategies they identified in Chapter 3 to ensure that their studies are credible (Are the findings trustworthy?), transferable (Can the findings be generalized?), dependable (Can the finding be replicated?), and confirmable (Is the research unbiased?). This can be presented in many ways. One is to include headings for Credibility, Transferability, Dependability, and Confirmability, discussing how each was met through study implementation. For example,

Credibility

To assure that the research findings were credible, I used prolonged engagement and observation in the field of study and member checking. Prolonged engagement and observation for this study involved me in interviewing participants in their homes over an extended period of time (3 months) for a total of three interviews each. Each interview lasted an average of 60 minutes, and as we spent more time together and built trust, participants seemed to relax more with each interview and offer more intimate information than before. Member checking was utilized by . . .

Transferability

Insights gleaned from the lived experiences of these participants may be similar to insights about other populations with similar experiences. One should consider the setting, participants, and their experiences before generalizing any findings. The themes and general summary about this phenomenon may offer insights for [insert appropriate audience here].

Dependability

A detailed explanation of this research process was provided and followed in order to maintain dependability of the study. Repeating the steps of this research for additional research into the same phenomenon within a similar context should yield comparable findings. I provided a detailed audit trail to replicate the study in Chapter 3 and followed each step as described.

Confirmability

To protect the research from personal bias, I noted possible areas of bias in Chapter 3 and utilized journaling to make my personal biases explicit and to anticipate projections in the quest for understanding. I concentrated on the lived experiences of participants throughout the constant emergence of distractions and biases. My consistent goal was to replace my conceptions at that time with more suitable ones through the process of reflection. Through journaling, I revised personal biases, and my biases created the questions necessary for thought revision (the hermeneutic circle). Every revision of a preconception projected a new meaning, and competing projections surfaced alongside each other until the agreement of meaning was clear.

Going Back to Chapter 3

At this point, students should return to Chapter 3: Methods and insert relevant quotes from Chapter 4: Results to illustrate their data analysis steps. This step is important because it allows the reader to understand how each step of the data analysis was completed through the findings. This step adds another layer of trustworthiness to the study (dependability) and allows others to replicate the study with greater certainty. Illustrations on how this might look are already provided in Chapter 3. To use the data example within this chapter, I provide a few examples below.

Illustrated Data Analysis Steps

The first step was to read each participant's interview transcript to understand the whole account of experience. After reading, I created preliminary "meaning units," from the elements in the transcript (Giorgi, 1985, p. 10) and focused on the topic of investigation. A meaning unit is the demarcated part of data that reveals a characteristic of the phenomenon being investigated. An example of the two preliminary units is illustrated from P1's description. The first meaning unit describes P1's disappointment about the sex in his marriage while the second meaning unit describes P1's expectation that sex would be like the sexual fantasies he created from pornography and television.

1. *"Intimacy with her wasn't what I thought it was going to be. At least from a physical standpoint."*

2. *"Now my fantasy and that assumption of what I am supposed to get from my spouse doesn't happen. So it wasn't realistic, my fantasies and what I expected from sex in my marriage."*

After this step, I obtained additional data by conducting individual follow-up interviews. I first identified gaps in the data (like unclear information or missing communication) in the initial transcript and created interview questions for each participant based on those gaps. I interviewed each participant for more illumination to fill each gap. I then transcribed each follow-up individual interview, read it, and integrated the information into the original analysis. This step also involved deleting irrelevant information or repetitive statements that were unnecessary for data analysis. An example of the edited synthesis is provided and illustrates this researcher's aim to identify a gap of information pertaining to "getting disgusted with myself." From this statement, the researcher seeks to clarify what P2 means by being disgusted with himself, as it could mean many things. The statements printed in bold font were obtained in the follow-up interview to clarify P2's initial statement.

P2:	One woman that was a wife of a friend would have inappropriate communications with me, and it would start out with, "Hey, how's the kids? What's going on?" whether it was a chat or an e-mail or whatever, and it would always turn to a sexual nature, and I would usually get disgusted with myself and shut it off. I think when you talk to sexual addicts, particularly those who are believers, you're not happy with yourself. There are some people that live in this lifestyle, and this is what they want, but for me, any event would bring guilt and shame.
I:	**You would feel guilt and shame because of your religious beliefs?**
P2:	**Absolutely, yes. I was wanting to be righteous, and I was wanting to be a good husband. I was wanting to be a good father. With this particular person, even though I came clean with everything else years ago, this particular person was some-one who was in the dark. I allowed that situation to stay in the dark, and it caused me guilt and shame and anger.**

The third step of data analysis was to . . .

SUMMARY

Students will keep the summary brief and purposeful. Discuss the main points of Chapter 4 and transition to Chapter 5. Continue to keep this portion of the chapter succinct. One paragraph is sufficient.

APPENDICES

Students will need to attach certain documents in the Appendix section of the dissertation, and many of those documents come from what is created in Chapter 3. In most cases, students will provide copies of the recruitment flyer (if applicable), screening tool, interview guide, and consent to participate. See the Appendix section of this book for some examples of these documents.

REFERENCES AND RESOURCES ——

Edger, K. (2009). Evangelical Christian men who identify as sexual addicts: An existential-phenomenological investigation. *Sexual Addiction and Compulsivity, 16*, 289–323.

Edger, K. (2011). *Losing the bond with God: Sexual addiction and evangelical men.* Santa Barbara, CA: Praeger.

Giorgi, A. (1985). Sketch of a psychological phenomenological method. In A. Giorgi (Ed.), *Phenomenology and psychological research* (pp. 8–22). Pittsburgh, PA: Duquesne University Press.

Heidegger, M. (1962). *Being and time.* New York, NY: Harper & Row.

Heidegger, M. (1971). *Poetry, language, thought.* New York, NY: Harper & Row.

Husserl, E. (1960). *Cartesian meditations: An introduction to phenomenology.* Boston, MA: Martinus Nijhoff.

Peoples, K. (2014). A phenomenological study: Evangelical Christian men who self-identify as sex addicts. *SAGE Research Methods Cases.* doi: 10.4135/978144627305014537190

Smith, D. W., & McIntyre, R. (1984). *Husserl and intentionality: A study of mind, meaning, and language.* Boston, MA: D. Reidel.

Wrathall, M. (2006). *How to read Heidegger.* New York, NY: W. W. Norton.

Discussion

The discussion section is such an important part of the dissertation because this is where students demonstrate their research proficiency. In the Discussion chapter, students present creative solutions to problems that are based on their research findings. They form a deeper understanding of the research problem and how their research findings are relevant to current research and their discipline of study. The main purpose of the discussion is to present how the findings of the study are significant in relation to what is already realized in scholarly literature. A student's aim is to present how the study propels the understanding of a research problem forward from what was presented in Chapter 1. The Discussion should be written in a funnel format, just like the literature review. Students should move from general to specific as they discuss their results in relation to their (1) literature reviews, moving to a discussion about interpreting findings in relation to their (2) phenomenological framework, and lastly, how their results speak to (3) application in their discipline. Chapter 5 is the least prescriptive chapter in terms of format. Discussion chapters are written in different ways and in different styles, but most have the basic elements discussed here.

Introduction

Students also should begin with concisely restating the purpose and nature of their study and why it was conducted. A brief summary of the study's key findings should also be presented here. Depending on the dissertation committee's expectations, a student may need to present a brief summary of what is presented in Chapter 5, but that is not always necessary.

Interpretation of Findings: A Dialogue With the Literature

When interpreting findings, students describe how their findings extend knowledge in their discipline of study and connect their results with their review of literature, creating a dialogue with the literature reviewed. The importance of connecting study results with the literature review is paramount because comparing and contrasting the findings of other studies reinforces the importance of the dissertation research and how it differs from other research of the topic. When summarizing key research findings, students should discuss if each set of results were either surprising or expected and why. Students will need to expand on results that were unexpected or especially insightful and discuss these results in relation to the problem statement. They also need to compare their research results with relevant studies presented in their literature reviews, highlighting only specific studies rather than every study presented in Chapter 2.

Including Theory Throughout

Students will analyze and interpret their research findings in the context of their chosen phenomenological framework (transcendental or hermeneutic). Some of the questions about the researcher's process can be answered in different sections, but the discussion about participants' process should be included in the Interpretation of Findings. Consider answering these questions for reporting theoretical implications when using transcendental phenomenology:

Discussing the Researcher's Process Within a Transcendental Theoretical Framework

Horizon—The horizon cannot be bracketed, so you will need to discuss that not everything could have been realized by you, the researcher. Discuss this in the Implications for Future Research section. Discuss what you may have missed due to your present experience (horizon) at the time you interviewed participants and analyzed data.

Bracketing—How was bracketing utilized in analyzing data and understanding the findings? This can be discussed in several sections in interpreting results.

Discussing Participants' Experiences Within a Transcendental Theoretical Framework

Horizon—What different horizons did you see throughout participants' experiences? During a participant's explanation of a present experience, what might you not have been able to see because of their current situatedness? Was there a realization later about certain ideas or understandings?

Intentionality—Identify examples of participants' intentionality. Intentionality is a participant's consciousness of something that is directed by his or her horizon of what something means or how something is perceived at that time.

Consider answering these questions for reporting theoretical implications when using hermeneutic phenomenology:

Discussing the Researcher's Process Within a Hermeneutic Theoretical Framework

Dasein—How has your *Dasein* affected the research? How did the research affect your *Dasein*, your being there? This could be included in the Limitations section.

Fore-Sight/Fore-Conception—What was your preconceived knowledge about the phenomenon you were studying?

Hermeneutic Circle—How were your understandings revised as you analyzed the data?

Discussing Participants' Experiences Within a Hermeneutic Theoretical Framework

Dasein—How were participants "being-in-the-world" with others? How did participants find themselves in situations that were not of their making? How did participants actualize their *Dasein* or fail to actualize?

Fore-Sight/Fore-Conception—What was participants' preconceived knowledge about certain experiences or situations and how did it change?

Hermeneutic Circle—How did participants revise their interpretations or understandings about different situations in their experiences?

Comparing dissertation findings to other research findings is fairly straightforward. Research findings may not always differ from earlier literature, but many researchers can usually point to a few contrasts in their findings, and those should be highlighted. For example,

Though some evangelicals question the claim that the woman was originally assigned a subsidiary status, many evangelicals place the male as the head of the house. Ongoing debates about gender roles and the hierarchical marital view of male over female continue among evangelicals (Grenz, 1997), perpetuating confusion over proper gender roles. In my research findings, I found that only half of my participants were confused over gender roles while the other half were grounded in the concept of the man being the head of the household.

Phenomenological research studies heavily lean on theoretical literature due to their exploratory nature and because there are often limited studies on certain topics. This is why it is so important to compare and contrast research findings to theoretical alongside content comparisons and contrasts. An example of how students can present their results in a dialogue with theoretical literature follows. I prefer the use of subheadings to organize the dialogue in a succinct manner:

In the following discussion, I present a dialogue with the Literature Review. Themes drawn from this study are compared and contrasted with findings from other studies to create a deeper understanding of the evangelical Christian male who identifies himself as a sexual addict.

Formalization of Christianity and the Loss of the God-bond

Jung's (1966) understanding that the lost bond with God is attributed to a formalized and institutionalized Christianity emerged throughout this the study. Participants felt that they had to live up to the stringent Biblical doctrine that their denominational understanding had formalized. To look at a woman with lust in one's heart was a sin and a disgrace, yet all participants failed to honor this doctrine in the way that they understood it dogmatically. The formalized understanding of God's rules caused all participants' initially established bonds with God to deteriorate in different ways; participants either completely abandoned their bond with God because of their immense guilt over lusting, or they developed a gradual detachment from God, shifting their God-bond from a personal relationship with a savior and spiritual confidant to an engagement with God as a confessional, a source for recurring forgiveness from ongoing sin. Some participants experienced a combination, praying to God to forgive them while simultaneously feeling overwhelmed by guilt and shame because of ongoing sexual behaviors.

The Shifting Evangelical Movement and the Concept of Absolute Truth

Evangelicalism continues to be better known for its internal differences rather than for its harmony despite a common doctrine, and while the evangelical spectrum spans from varying degrees of conservative stances to more liberal understandings, many evangelicals continue to stand by their individual understanding of dogma as the only truth (Barrett, 2001). For many of the participants in this study, individual evangelical stances shifted from understanding God through stringent dogmatic principles to a more lenient understanding of God, a God that was sympathetic to the inherent fallen condition of the human being, and therefore accepting, patient, and forgiving. For these participants, the understanding of God shifted from God as judge to God as mentor. God as mentor has a significantly different role from the previous understanding of God (judge), and it enabled participants to alter their relationship with God. Since the evangelical movement encompasses varying religious stances on dogma that are based on social and cultural understandings, this allowed the participants within this movement to shift their spiritual understandings to suit their personal life-worlds while still remaining within the universal and mutual evangelical doctrine.

Sexual Morality and Sexual Addiction

Throughout history, Christian views about sexual morality changed depending on the dogma of the Christian institution. Evangelicals rejected the concept that sex was to be engaged in only for procreation and celebrated sexuality as the need to be fruitful and multiply (Grenz, 1997; Horowitz, 2002). As the emphasis on euphoria of sex heightened through the Enlightenment and into this century, evangelicals rebelled against the growing emphasis on the primacy of sexual pleasure, creating a renewed concept of sexual morality, a morality that is largely conservative and based on a celibate life until marriage. Though all participants in this study engaged in sexual activities for pleasure, including emotional affirmation as well as carnal gratification, all participants' beliefs about sexual morality did not waver. Even as their understanding of God changed, sex was still viewed the same way throughout, as a union that is permitted only within a heterosexual marriage. Lusting, defined as a sexual craving of something forbidden by God (Harris, 2003; Harris, 2004) continued to be understood as a sin that should be avoided at all costs. Participants were continually conflicted by their sexual urges even from young ages. The childhood sexual exploration was often turned to shame. As participants yearned to explore their bodies through masturbation and sexual relationships, the concept of sinful lust conflicted with the freedom to explore their sexuality. Participants would often hide their behaviors from others because they felt what they were doing was wrong or not normal, despite ongoing urges. Though all participants continued to lust, whether by looking at women or through pornography, they now depended on treatment-based or 12 Step regimens to help them change their thinking through cognitive dissonance activities. All participants were introduced to the concept of sexual addiction through evangelical self-help literature (predominantly Every Man's Battle) and 12 step programs (Sexaholics Anonymous) and only then identified as sexual addicts. All participants reported ongoing struggles with lust even throughout years of participation in their self-help programs. The need to surrender to self-help structures to curb the inherent experience of lusting may be a dependent cycle since guilt about lusting, for all participants, has been a recurring emotion throughout their lives. Kwee's (2007) notion that individuals may view unwanted sexual attractions as sicknesses because of their inability to stop those attractions while simultaneously being dependent on self-help structures parallels the experiences of the participants in this study. Since sexual lust is an inherent emotion with its initial exploration in childhood, can it ever be eliminated from one's life, and if it cannot, does the self-help structure that claims that emotion as wrong encourage dependence on it through the sheer male inability to stop lusting? It has seemed to be the case for the participants of this study.

While sexual addiction is rooted in shame, religious dogma often contributes to the shame cycle. Out of fear and condemnation, individuals may hide certain kinds of sexual behaviors or urges that are viewed as sinful and isolate themselves (Nelson, 2003). Participants in this study created three life-worlds where they were able to isolate themselves when they engaged in certain behaviors that did not fit into their other life-worlds. Participants had convinced themselves that they could not change, and so they tried to escape from the distressful uncertainties of their lives by creating compartmentalized life-worlds, paralleling Fischer's (1985) concept of self-deception as the "flight from the anxiously distressing ambiguities of one's life" (p. 152).

Gender Roles

Ongoing debates about gender roles and the hierarchical marital view of male over female continue among evangelicals (Grenz, 1997), and though some evangelicals question the claim that the woman was originally assigned a subsidiary status, most conservative evangelicals ignore the argument and place the male as the head of the house. Exactly how that male is supposed to function as leader, however, is widely disputed and seems to be dependent on individual interpretation. Most participants in this study felt that they had to be leaders of their households, yet they did not know how to lead and how to interact with their families as leaders, and they did not receive any specific religious guidance about such leadership. Participants understood it as their Biblical expectation but did not know exactly how to carry out the role. Contention grew between husband and wife because wives often felt that their husbands did not fulfill their leadership roles appropriately, and participants grew frustrated with their marriages and frequently felt inadequate as men. Their extramarital sexual behaviors allowed them to escape and to feel validated as men. After the participants decided to obtain help for their sexual behaviors and aligned with a recovery program, many still saw a need to establish their role as leader of the house and worked with their spouses to shape that role. Others considered their spouses primary leaders and did not feel responsible for being the heads of their households. Despite the categorization of male as leader or female as leader, each participant's leader role varied greatly from the other. Where one participant divided leadership roles with his wife, financial responsibilities being male and caring for children being female, another participant understood his role as being a supporter of his wife while another participant became a spiritual witness to his wife and his child.

The Saving Grace of Marriage

The importance placed on waiting to have sex until marriage is still a strong case in evangelical literature (Alcorn, 2003; Elliot, 2006; Graham, 1984; Gresh, 2007; Harris, 2003; Harris, 2004), while the marital bond is often described in a fairytale manner, as is the case in Gresh's (2007) description of her marriage being "more than [they] hoped for" (p. 14). The idealization of marriage was also present in most of the study's participants' experiences. Marriage was seen as something that would eliminate their lustful urges for other women as well as their sexual urges caused by pornographic images. They felt that they would be emotionally, sexually, and spiritually fulfilled when they met their wives and that marriage would end all of their problems. When that did not happen, problems arose, resentments grew, and often blaming behaviors began. Many men blamed their wives for not meeting their sexual urges, and they seemed to have fashioned sexual roles for their wives prior to meeting them. The expectations participants placed on their future wives paralleled the roles that are fashioned for women in much of the evangelical literature where the wife's responsibility is to satisfy her husband's sexual urges (Dobson, 1980; Morgan 1990; White, 1993), possibly contributing to the unrealistic expectation that one's partner is solely responsible for meeting one's sexual needs, as frequent or as extravagant as they may be. The hierarchical role placed on women to honor their husbands could also have been a significant factor in participants' blaming behaviors since hierarchical gender role duties often tend to contribute to blaming when assigned or presumed gender roles are not being executed by the individuals who were prescribed those roles (Laaser & Gregoire, 2003).

Homosexuality and the Evangelical Sex Addict

All of the participants stated that they were heterosexual men and that they did not engage in any homosexual acts. All of these men stated that they thought homosexuality and sexual addiction were similar since both were problematic in an evangelical Christian life. Since this study focused primarily on men who identified as heterosexual, more investigation needs to be done on evangelical Christian men who identify as homosexual. Questions still remain as to how much of this population, evangelical Christian men who identify as sexual addicts, identify homosexual desires and acts as addictive or problematic. I wonder if or how many homosexual evangelical Christian men who feel that they are sexually addicted work toward a healthier same-sex union. How much of this population identifies homosexuality as problematic and moves toward reform or celibacy and how much of this population separates sexual addiction from same-sex desires? While reforming homosexual desires is controversial, it was an aspect that was mentioned when homosexuality was discussed with these participants because lust and same-sex attractions were viewed as the same problems. In terms of lust, all participants stated that they continued to struggle with lusting after females even years into their recovery journeys. Many were convinced that lusting would be a life-long struggle that they would need to battle. Since same-sex sexual thoughts and actions are sinful within the conservative evangelical community (Banerjee, 2005), being unable to stop homosexual desires would be irrelevant within the evangelical culture because just as any lust is sinful despite an inability to stop, acting on homosexual desires is sinful too. The ability to just stop being gay is irrelevant. Since all lust is sinful and homosexuality is sinful within this dogma, both straight and gay evangelical Christian men need to either remain celibate or stay within the boundaries of a monogamous heterosexual union.

Reaction Formation

Evangelicalism has been characterized as a hypocritical institution (Gamson, 2001) quite possibly because of past sex scandals of evangelists like Ted Haggard (same-sex scandal) and Jimmy Swaggart (opposite-sex scandal). One may wonder if unfavorable sexual behaviors could be linked to evangelical leadership by way of reaction formation. Reaction formation is a defense mechanism where anxious or unwanted feelings are replaced by other feelings that are deemed more appropriate and where the consequence of this switch is obsessional behavior (Freud, 2000). In my research, all participants were church leaders with roles like mentors (P1), speakers (P2), elders (P3 and P6), Sunday school pastors (P4), and deacons (P5) while using their leadership positions to feel righteous during the time of their sexual indiscretions.

Jean-Paul Sartre stated that psychoanalytic language often inhibited the understanding of phenomena and that people and their issues were really the results of their lived environments (1984). In my study, the participants' lived environments affected them in terms of exhibiting reaction formation behaviors. Quite interestingly, even though all of the participants were church leaders, none of them chose to be leaders on their own. P1 was approached by many men in his church who asked him to speak publicly. P2 and P6 were both asked by many to be elected as elders and P5 as a deacon. P4 was asked to pastor Sunday school by his church leaders. Hence, in many ways, the participants' environments in church invoked many honorable characteristics on these men, which created a reaction formation parallel that was participatory in nature.

Sartre and Personal Responsibility

The impossibility of escaping one's one responsibility (Sartre, 1984) was an emerging theme for all participants in this study. Initially, participants depended on God to take their urges away, and when God failed them, they felt victimized. They did not understand why they were burdened with lustful feelings and why they could not stop themselves from acting out. Participants felt that it was God's responsibility to correct their behavior or redeem them of it. God's unwillingness to lift their sexual burdens enabled participants to understand themselves as victims, helpless in the face of lust and powerless to stop their behaviors. Though guilt and shame were oppressing for some, placing the responsibility on God to change them enabled participants to continue their behaviors. Each participant's choice to hold on to his sexual world was made possible through choosing not to change his current situation, and this choice was rationalized through the victim role created by the understanding that God failed him. Only after participants were exposed and faced with considerable consequences did participants choose to make another choice—reform.

Becker and Three Life-Worlds

Becker (1973) stated that people with sexual issues wanted and attempted to be whole, and that the sought wholeness is ontological in nature instead of sexual. People strive to feel complete within themselves and to be at one with their life-worlds. Participants in my research had difficulty feeling wholeness due to their sexual feelings and indiscretions since their sexual yearnings clashed with their Christian beliefs. As they engaged in illicit sexual acts, they clung to their Christian value systems, which did not approve of what they were doing. Consequently, they gradually separated their life-world, dividing it between a religious-world and an illicit sexual-world. In their striving for ontological wholeness, many participants depended on God to take away their sexual-world, and after God's consistent failure, marriage was looked at as their salvation from conflicting life-worlds. After they were married, participants believed that their secret sexual-worlds would cease to exist because their wives would enter that sexual role and their sexual behaviors would be dogmatically legitimate. When wives failed to accomplish this goal, participants created a third world, their marriage-world, a world that did not harmonize with their spiritual world because of its flaws (blaming, fighting, lying, etc.), flaws that were often created or exacerbated by each participant's choice to remain in the secret sexual-world.

Assumptions

Students will discuss their assumptions in this section as well. What assumptions were present, and how were they either suspended if using Husserl or revised in using Heidegger? Below is an example of two ways a student could write about how assumptions played a part in their analysis and their reflection on changed points of view.

For a transcendental phenomenological dissertation (Husserl), a student would discuss assumptions within the data. Since all prior assumptions would have been suspended, the focus of addressing assumptions would be about assumptions or, better yet, information that the researcher found interesting or surprising within the data only. For example, a participant may have stated one thing and done another. This would lead a transcendental phenomenological researcher to say "hmm." No previous assumptions would be included because they would have already been suspended.

For a hermeneutic phenomenological dissertation (Heidegger), a student would discuss how previous assumptions were revised with the data that were analyzed. Prior assumptions may have been noted in a journal or within Chapter 3 of the dissertation. A student would need to address those previous assumptions in this section and discuss how those assumptions were either revised or confirmed.

Addressing conceptual assumptions (Husserl)

The primary attitude I maintained throughout the data analysis process was one of curiosity. Any biases about this population were set aside, bracketed. If an assumption surfaced about a participant or participants, I asked participants directly about my query so as to not assume anything. In every point of the analysis process, the data had to speak for themselves. If presented information elicited a certain understanding for me but was not concretely demonstrated in the data, I went back to participants with clarifying questions to verify (or contradict) the understanding through participants' testimonies rather than my own understandings. My most interesting finding was that all participants served in leadership roles in their religious-worlds. Reaction formation was evident for all participants, though most participants increased their involvement in their churches through hierarchy (spiritual leader for others) rather than volume (attending church more often). I was very intrigued when I found out that all participants chose to remain married; of course, this could have been purely coincidental due to the small sample size. That participants chose to remain married was not as interesting as the nature of some participants' current marital relationships. That participants accepted that they may never be trusted again by their spouses was a fascinating finding since they discussed how important it was to have trust in their marriages.

As I analyzed participants' narratives, I also discovered that most participants were conservative evangelicals and viewed homosexual behaviors as unacceptable. Most participants discussed their disapproval of homosexual behaviors except P6, who went to church with a homosexual male couple and was hesitant to judge the couple as sinful. In analyzing this phenomenon, I followed up with P6 with an interview to ask why he did not seem to judge the homosexual couple in his church as sinful. P6 stated that it was not his place to judge others. He had done things that were sinful in the eyes of God as well, and God should be his only judge. From his answer, I found out that P6's restraint of judgment of this couple was the result of his tacit desire that his own sexual behavior was not judged by others. His guilt about his illicit sexual affairs had an impact on how he looked at others whom he might normally condemn under the guidance of strict evangelical doctrine. This was different from the other participants, who noted that homosexuality was sinful and unacceptable in the eyes of God, and I found it noteworthy. Another finding I found interesting was that while the data showed that marital stressors exacerbated participants' ongoing sexual behaviors, stress of the marital relationship was not the causal factor of participants' sexual behaviors. Most participants experienced feelings of inadequacy and used sex to feel better about themselves, and this was the beginning process to their illicit affairs. Problems in participants' marriages often arose because of their secretive sexual behaviors, and marriage stress was not evidenced to be the causal factor of participants' sexual behaviors. While participants discussed having fairly rigid belief systems about what sexuality is and how sexuality should look like in the eyes of God, the rigidity regarding sexuality was not a consistent component across all participants' experiences, and I found this interesting because of the evangelical's personal relationship with God and because all participants stated that they strived to live within God's expectations. Lastly, only two of the six participants sought church guidance for sexual issues despite all participants stating that they were active participants in their churches and that they formed deep relationships with congregants and church leaders. So I found it interesting that while they deemed themselves to be such active participants, they were largely separate in terms of seeking help or counsel from their church communities.

Revising Conceptual Assumptions (Heidegger)

My first assumption was that most participants would be conservative evangelicals and view homosexual behaviors as unacceptable. This assumption was validated as participants discussed their disapproval of homosexual behaviors. P6, however, went to church with a homosexual male couple, and his hesitancy to judge the couple as sinful was surprising to me. I looked over P6's narrative after discovering this finding, and a new conception arouse. Based on the narrative P6 presented, it is likely that P6's restraint of judgment of this couple was the result of his tacit desire that his own sexual behavior not be judged by others. His guilt about his illicit sexual affairs had an impact on how he looked at others whom he might normally condemn under the guidance of strict evangelical doctrine. Another presupposition was that some of the participants would have had significant stress in their marital relationships prior to exhibiting sexual addictive behaviors. Many participants exhibited compulsive sexual behavior prior to their marriages, so the stress of the marital relationship was not the causal factor of participants' sexual behaviors. Most participants experienced feelings of inadequacy and used sex to help them feel more adequate, and this was the beginning process of their illicit affairs. Problems in participants' marriages often arose because of their secretive sexual behaviors, and marriage stress was not evidenced to be the causal factor of participants' sexual behaviors. However, marital stressors exacerbated participants' ongoing sexual behaviors. Participants were also assumed to have fairly rigid belief systems about what sexuality should look like in the eyes of God. While some participants discussed being raised in religious families, the rigidity regarding sexuality was not a consistent factor across all participants' experiences. The factor that was consistent in all participants' family lives, however, was the emotional absence of a parent. The concept of absent fathers as a factor in helping evangelical men battle sexual addiction is quite present in programs such as Promise Keepers (through healing "father wounds"), yet it was somehow a new discovery to me, and I found this fascinating. Perhaps I did not expect that "father wounds" were legitimate or I disregarded the validity of evangelical programs such as Promise Keepers. This new conception showed me prior blatant disregard for the validity of programs within the evangelical community. In my research, five participants discussed their experiences of having an absent father, and one discussed an absent mother. While some participants experienced chaotic or abusive family lives, the existence of a chaotic or abusive family upbringing could not be generalized to all participants' childhood experiences. I also presumed that participants would have a pattern of consistently seeking guidance of their church leaders on sexual matters, and this was not often the case. Only two of the six participants sought church guidance for sexual issues. Others depended solely on their dogmatic concept of sexual morality. My assumption that participants would have confusion over gender roles was evidenced in only half of the participants' experiences, but reaction formation as a contributive factor was present for all participants. The primary postulation that my initial assumptions would be challenged and/ or altered by hearing participants' lived experiences was present. I kept an open attitude to revising my belief system about this population, and I fully expected that my understanding of this group would change. My most surprising finding was that all participants served in leadership roles in their religious-worlds. Though the assumption of reaction formation was certainly present, I assumed that most participants would increase their involvement in their churches in terms of volume (attending church more often) rather than hierarchy (spiritual leader for others). The final unexpected finding was that all participants chose to remain married; of course, this could have been purely coincidental due to the small sample size. That participants chose to remain married did not astonish me as much as the nature of some participants' current marital relationships. It would be expected that all marriages would experience difficulty in healing because of participants' infidelities, but that participants accepted that they may never be trusted again by their spouses was an unforeseen finding. Though all participants admitted to having ongoing problems in their marriages (except P5, who was vague in his answers on this topic), some participants' marital relationships seemed exceptionally malevolent.

How to Create a Quality Interpretation of Findings

- Are findings discussed in terms of how they extend knowledge in the discipline of study?
- Are study results connected with the review of literature?
- Is there a discussion of each set of results and whether they were surprising or expected and why?
- Are results that were unexpected or especially insightful expanded upon? Are they discussed in relation to the problem statement?
- Is there a comparison of research results with relevant studies presented in the literature reviews, highlighting only specific studies?
- Are theoretical topics addressed in the dialogue with literature?
- Are research findings interpreted in the context of the study's phenomenological framework (transcendental or hermeneutic)?

Limitations

No research is perfect, and all human subjects research have limitations. When students identify potential limitations of their dissertation research, they should discuss them succinctly and in relative importance to the overall interpretation of the results. Perhaps the number of participants was small and may not be generalizable to a larger population. Generalizability and a small participant pool will be the case for nearly every phenomenological study, and, of course, generalizability is not the purpose of a phenomenological study. However, many universities and committee members may want this noted anyway despite its not being a noteworthy limitation, so it is important to mention here.

Perhaps certain questions were not asked and could have revealed more information about a phenomenon. Some limitations may have influenced qualitative rigor, but those limitations do not always exist in all research projects, so students need not be pressed to find weaknesses that affect the qualitative rigor of results. It is important to be self-critical and honest about one's research limitations without being defensive or apologetic. Avoid sentence like, "This was a limitation of my research, but the reason I did it this way was because . . ." Just state the limitations and how they might have affected the results. No apologies necessary. For example,

There was no racial diversity in this study because all of the participants were Caucasian. Hence, this study is limited in terms of answering questions about the interplay of race in the lived experiences of evangelical Christian men identifying as sexually addicted.

Recommendations for Future Research

In this section, students need to discuss possible implications of their research in other areas of study and consider viable amendments for future research development. Recommendations for future research should be grounded in the literature review as well as in the strengths and limitations of the dissertation study. All recommendations should be kept within the boundaries of the dissertation study. Students should not make recommendations for future research that are based upon their assumptions or convictions (ex: Future research should address how the evangelical church is working with the spouses of evangelical sexual addicts because they are clearly suffering in the marriage, even after the truth is discovered.). All research recommendations should be grounded in the context of the findings in their particular study (ex: Further research on this topic would be useful in illuminating this population's motivations for continuing married life with distrusting partners even after years of recovery work. The reciprocal of that research would be to illuminate the spouses' reasons for staying in a marriage after finding out about sexual indiscretions.). Students may discuss what they learned in their dissertation study as they propose recommendations to help improve future research or best practices in the field of study. Two more examples below demonstrate these guidelines:

Recommendation Based on Something Learned

It was interesting that all of the participants chose to work on their marriages with their betrayed spouses even after notable long-term struggles over a period of years, predominantly with trust. Gender differences exist in relation to how spouses deal with jealousy after infidelity, and those differences were evident in this study. Further phenomenological research on this topic would be useful in illuminating men's reasons for staying married after infidelity and women's reasons for staying in marriages after infidelity when they are the injured party.

Recommendation Based on Limitation of Research

The research participants were limited to a demographic within one geographical location. It would be beneficial to collect data from participants across different geographical locations and different ethnicities to enhance richness of the findings of this study.

Implications

In this section, students will need to highlight the importance of the dissertation study and how it contributes to filling gaps in current research literature. Students may also have discovered additional gaps that were not formerly uncovered or sufficiently explained in literature. Recommendations for practice and/or social change should be discussed here along with any methodological and theoretical implications. Headings can be used to clarify each implication. The example below demonstrates an implication for social change:

This dissertation study illustrated several problems that educators face in terms of daily stress and work culture. A possible approach to helping educators decrease stress in the work setting would be to rely on principles associated with Paulo Freire (1985). Freire's concept of conscientization ("the process by which human beings participate critically in a transforming act," p. 106) can be used to restructure the education system. Freire believed that ruling classes were incapable of freeing the oppressed. Hence, the educational system cannot be freed by administrators or government. Beneficial change of work culture can occur only through a grassroots movement by way of collaboration of educators, administrators, and students to change an oppressive educational system.

Conclusion
••

Students may want to include a succinct review of the key implications of the study along with an explanation about the importance of the research findings and how they contribute to current research literature and the field of practice. Recommendations for further research that illustrate that data have been examined adequately can conclude this section. Above all, the good conclusion provides a strong message or lesson that captures the spirit of the study, a take-home message. For example,

Through this investigation, I provided a detailed analysis of the life-world of this population through corporeal, temporal, spatial, and relational reflections. Evangelical men struggled with sexual behaviors because they yearned for illicit sexual gratification while also yearning to follow God's expectations. Despite the rules placed upon them by their dogma and their church leaders, these men chose to live parallel lives but sensed that they were powerless and could not take control of their lives. They lived parallel lives until it became too much or until they were caught and addressed their problematic behaviors, only later taking personal responsibility for their behaviors, which liberated them. It is my hope that counselors understand the importance of placing their clients as the primary controllers of their decisions while simultaneously helping them change past detrimental decision-making patterns into more beneficial decision-making patterns. After all, life inherently limits possibilities. When working with evangelical men who struggle with sexual behaviors that they find problematic, counselors can confront clients with the notion that when they make one choice, they essentially give up other choices, and therefore, a compromise is essential (between their urges and the consequences of acting on those urges). Clients can choose to live the lives they desire but only within the limitations of existence. It is my hope that counselors will find useful information from this investigation in helping this population, particularly through the notion that individuals are always in the world and in the circumstances of existence (Heidegger, 1962), searching for wholeness (Becker, 1973), and always personally responsible for their lives (Sartre, 1984).

Update the Abstract

If students have followed my book step by step, they are now at the end and ready to submit the dissertation. After a dissertation is submitted for formal review by the committee (and any other reviewers depending on each student's university process), an oral dissertation defense follows. But before submitting the dissertation document for review, students need to update the Abstract to introduce the entire dissertation. Include information from Chapters 4 and 5, change future tense to past tense where appropriate, and stay within maximum word count (universities vary). A dissertation abstract looks like this:

Abstract

This is the abstract, which is typed in block format with no indentation. It should be accurate and concise. Your abstract should also be written in a self-contained way so people reading only your abstract would fully understand the content and the implications of your dissertation. Write this section last when you have collected all the information in your proposal. Your abstract is a short summary of your entire dissertation and is not a statement of what readers should expect to read in your dissertation. Your committee members should be able to read the abstract and know what your proposal discusses. Avoid sentences like "This dissertation proposal will . . ."

Keywords: research, literature, methods, limitations

Example of Abstract

Abstract

Issues of sexual addiction have swept the evangelical movement, and ongoing concerns in the evangelical community are evidenced by its self-help literature, men's movements, and sex manuals. The purpose of this study was to illuminate the lived experiences of evangelical Christian men identified as being sexually addicted. This qualitative method was existential-phenomenological and focused on the lived experiences of this population. Individual interviews of six evangelical men who identified as sexual addicts were analyzed. In the results of this study, it was found that this population lives life among compartmentalized worlds. Three worlds emerged: the religious-world, the marital-world, and the sexual-world. It is only through forced merging of these three worlds, which happens through exposure and the threat of extreme consequences, that this population submits to change. When sexually addicted evangelical Christian men submit to changing their ways, they take comfort in the sexual addiction label because they can identify with others in the evangelical Christian community who also utilize this label. Hence, this label of sexual addiction identifies them as in need of help and gives them relief as they grow dependent on recovery programs and experience a renewed dedication and understanding of God. The results of this study show a need for counselors working with this population on recovery efforts to realize that there is an inextricable link between the choices made in life and one's relationship with God.

Keywords: evangelical men, Christian men, sexual addiction, phenomenological

REFERENCES AND RESOURCES

Barrett, D. V. (2001). *The new believers: Sects, "cults" and alternative religions.* New York, NY: Sterling.

Freire, P. (1985). *The politics of education.* Westport, CT: Bergin & Garvey.

Goodson, P. (2017). Exercises for writing the discussion or conclusions section. In P. Goodson, *Becoming an academic writer: 50 exercises for paced, productive, and powerful writing* (2nd ed., Chap. 10). Thousand Oaks, CA: Sage.

Jung, C. G. (1966). *Psychology and religion.* Binghamton, NY: The Vail-Ballou Press. (Original work published 1936)

References From Examples

Alcorn, R. (2003). *The purity principle: God's safeguards for life's dangerous trails.* New York, NY: Multnomah.

Banerjee, N. (2006, December 12). Gay and evangelical, seeking paths of acceptance. *The New York Times.* Retrieved from http://www.nytimes.com/2006/12/12/us/12evangelical.html

Barrett, D. V. (2001). *The new believers: Sects, "cults" and alternative religions.* New York, NY: Sterling.

Becker, E. (1973). *The denial of death.* New York, NY: Macmillan.

Dobson, J. (1980). *Preparing for adolescence.* Ventura, CA: Regal Books.

Edger, K. (2011). *Losing the bond with God: Sexual addiction and evangelical men.* Santa Barbara, CA: Praeger.

Edger, K. (2009). Evangelical Christian men who identify as sexual addicts: An existential-phenomenological investigation. *Sexual Addiction and Compulsivity, 16,* 289–323.

Elliot, E. (2006). *Passion and purity: Learning to bring your love life under Christ's control.* Grand Rapids, MI: Fleming H. Revell.

Fischer, W. F. (1985). Self-deception: An empirical-phenomenological inquiry into its essential meanings. In A. Giorgi (Ed.), *Phenomenology and psychological research.* (pp. 118–154). Pittsburgh, PA: Duquesne University Press.

Freud, S. (2000). *Three essays on the theory of sexuality.* New York. NY: Basic Books. (Original work published 1905)

Gamson, J. (2001). Normal sins: Sex scandal narratives as institutional morality tales. *Social Problems, 48,* 185–205.

Graham, B. (1984). *A biblical standard for evangelists.* Minneapolis, MN: Worldwide Productions.

Grenz, S. J. (1997). *Sexual ethics: An evangelical perspective.* Louisville, KY: Westminster John Knox Press.

Grenz, S. J. (1998). *Welcoming but not affirming: An evangelical response to homosexuality.* Louisville, KY: Westminster John Knox Press.

Gresh, D. (2007). *And the bride wore white: Seven secrets to sexual purity.* Chicago, IL: Moody.

Harris, J. (2006). *Sex is not the problem (lust is): Sexual purity in a lust-saturated world: Study guide for men.* New York, NY: Multnomah Books.

Harris, J. (2004). *Sex is not the problem (lust is): Sexual purity in a lust-saturated world: Study guide for women.* New York, NY: Multnomah Books.

Heidegger, M. (1962). *Being and time.* New York, NY: Harper & Row.

Horowitz, H. L. (2001). *Rereading sex: Battles over sexual knowledge and suppression in nineteenth-century America.* New York, NY: Alfred A. Knopf.

Jung, C. G. (1966). *Psychology and religion.* Binghamton, NY: The Vail-Ballou Press. (Original work published 1936)

Kwee, A. W., Dominguez, A.W., & Ferrell, D. (2007). Sexual addiction and Christian college men: Conceptual, assessment, and treatment challenges. *Journal of Psychology and Christianity, 26,1,* 3–13.

Laaser, M. R., & Gregoire, L. J. (2003). Pastors and cybersex addiction. *Sexual and Relationship Therapy, 18,* 395–404.

Morgan, M. (1975). *The total woman: How to make your marriage come alive.* New York, NY: Pocket Books.

Nelson, L. (2003). Sexual addiction versus sexual anorexia and the church's impact. *Sexual Addiction and Compulsivity, 10,* 179–191.

Sartre, J.-P. (1984). *Being and nothingness.* New York, NY: Washington Square Press. (Original work published 1943)

White, J. (1993). *Eros redeemed: Breaking the stronghold of sexual sin.* Downers Grove, IL: InterVarsity Press.

PART

After Your
Dissertation

CHAPTER
6

Other Phenomenological Methods

Three major disciplines exist within the Western tradition of phenomenology: transcendental phenomenology, hermeneutic phenomenology, and existential phenomenology. Yet human experiences are so diverse, as are researchers, so much that the three main phenomenological methods cannot satisfy the expectations of every research study. There have to be room for other modes of phenomenological inquiries, and many researchers have created their own phenomenological methods just for these reasons.

For the purpose of this book, which is explicitly for the dissertation student just learning about the process of phenomenological research, I focused only on transcendental and hermeneutic phenomenological research traditions, the philosophical traditions of Husserl and Heidegger applied in research. Most other phenomenological methodologies use a mix of philosophers with either Husserl or Heidegger as a foundation, and students new to phenomenological method are often overwhelmed and confused by the grand scope of options in phenomenological research. In fact, most of my students initially choose phenomenological texts that use a mix of philosophers when they begin their dissertation process simply because of their popularity. Being novices, they do not see a difference between interpretative phenomenological analysis and van Manen's reflective phenomenology. Isn't it all the same thing? Of course not, but how would a novice know? Hence, this is why I felt it pertinent to include this chapter for novice readers.

Alternative phenomenological methods that focus on rich descriptions of lived experience and meaning but do not strictly adhere to only Husserl or Heidegger allow researchers to use various phenomenological traditions and philosophies that work for their way of understanding and interpreting the world around them. While existential phenomenology falls in the "mixed" category of phenomenological method, it is such a major method that I felt it deserved special attention and used it to introduce the following list of methods. All other phenomenological methodologies are listed alphabetically after existential phenomenology, including methods that do not use Husserlian or Heideggerian philosophies. Following are some of these methods:

Existential Phenomenology

Existentialism stems from Blaise Pascal's (1623–1662) denunciation of Cartesian rationalism, which was a tradition that defined people within a rational scope. Pascal rejected this purely rational focus because he believed that people were more complex. They were both mind and body; more specifically, Pascal believed that people were a contradiction between mind and body. Søren Kierkegaard (1813–1855) was a Danish philosopher, a theologian, and a poet who was deemed to be the first existentialist philosopher. He agreed with Pascal's view of this contradictory characteristic within people. Kierkegaard (1988) believed that people became their true selves after they passed through three stages (the aesthetic stage that is ruled by passion, the ethical stage that is ruled by societal expectations, and the religious stage that is ruled by faith in God) and that all three stages competed and conflicted with one another. Existentialist-phenomenologists did not like to label themselves but are identified as part of this tradition because of their commonalities in their discussions about how to understand phenomena. For example, all existential phenomenologists agree that philosophy is subjective and should not be conducted from a disengaged position because phenomena often appear to a person who is engaged in the world (Warthall, 2006). Also, all existential-phenomenologists reject Husserl's idea of reductionism and emphasize portrayals of everyday experience to reach an understanding of phenomena. Key figures in existential phenomenology are Edmund Husserl, Max Scheler, Karl Jaspers, Gabriel Marcel, Martin Heidegger, Jean-Paul Sartre, Maurice Merleau-Ponty, and Paul Ricoeur (von Eckartsberg, 1998a). Existential-phenomenological research was created at Duquesne University in Pittsburgh, Pennsylvania. It is understood that existential-phenomenological researchers are never completely objective but that they are responsible for explaining their approach of inquiry in painstaking detail so that the connection between the researcher and the phenomenon is clear enough for readers to assess the validity of the research. Two basic approaches exist in existential-phenomenological research: empirical phenomenological and hermeneutical phenomenological. Empirical phenomenological methods focus on the general meaning of a phenomenon to answer the research question. Basically, what is this phenomenon (von Eckartsberg, 1998b)? Hermeneutical phenomenological methods focus on human experiences as they are expressed in spontaneous speech, in writing, or in art and view human experiences as texts that are awaiting interpretation (von Eckartsberg, 1998b). Hermeneutical methods are less structured and vary widely in approach.

Critical Narrative Analysis (Langdridge)

Critical narrative analysis (CNA) is primarily grounded in the works of Paul Ricoeur and Hans Gadamer. Ricoeur believed that constructing meaning through language was essential in phenomenological social psychology, and both Gadamer and Ricoeur emphasized the fact that language, more specifically, conversation, facilitated the understanding of experiences. Both believed that conversation (discourse) was the primary way to understand phenomena. Ricoeur differentiated between discourse and language. Discourse was spoken speech, and language was the system that fabricated discourse. Written discourse was termed *text* by Ricoeur, and he believed that text was no longer bound by human beings. Hence, text needs to be interpreted (hermeneutics) in order to generate understanding (Ricoeur, 1981). In interpreting text, researchers using this methodology focus on storytelling as well as criticism or skepticism. This is how CNA differs from other methods of narrative analysis; the researcher uses suspicion to understand the narratives. This hermeneutic phenomenological approach can be complex, grounded in the phenomenological tradition and modern developments of critical social theory, making it a critical social psychology (Langdridge, 2008).

Dialogal Approach (Halling, Leifer, & Rowe)

The dialogal research approach is grounded in the theory of dialogal phenomenology (Strasser, 1969). This type of research method is unique in that it is team based and does not require researchers to follow specific steps and procedures. When using this method, a group of researchers work together to discover a particular phenomenon in a collaborative way. Data analysis is collaborative and requires a phenomenological attitude, but no specific steps or text units are involved in the analysis process (Halling, Leifer, & Rowe, 2006). Accuracy of data analysis is promoted through an open dialogue among the researchers in how they relate to the data and by discussing their various perspectives in a team setting.

Dallas Approach (Garza)

The Dallas research approach was created at the University of Dallas and stems from the Duquesne University's existential-phenomenological research approach. The Dallas approach has three basic elements at its foundation to practice research: (1) co-constitution, (2) intentionality, and (3) life-world (Garza, 2007). The concept of co-constitution is that person who perceives (the researcher) participates in and even co-authors what is being perceived. Co-constitution is a bond between the researcher and the lived world and what is discovered in research is essentially subjective because the meaning of a phenomenon is unique to that researcher. Intentionality is, of course, the fundamental property of consciousness of looking at something according to Husserl. It is our awareness of something. Lastly, the world of phenomena is the life-world, the interactions people have between themselves and what they perceive along with the world of experienced horizons that we share with others (von Eckartsberg, 1998a). This belief is rooted in Husserl's concept of intentionality (Garza, 2007).

Embodied Life-World Approach (Todres)

Embodied interpretation is a research tradition belonging to a growing practice called aesthetic phenomenology where research is written in poetic and evocative ways. The embodied life-world is rooted in the works of Gadamer and Gendlin and was developed so that health care professionals could become more sensitized to people living with various health-related conditions (Todres & Galvin, 2008). This method depends on understanding phenomena through words and how they are felt in one's body. Gendlin (1978) believed that the understanding of a phenomenon as a whole is carried in the body. Researchers using this approach aim to communicate embodied understanding to readers by (1) finding their own bodily understanding of the whole and the parts of an interpreted experience and (2) sharing their insights in evocative ways that can bring the meanings of a phenomenon to life for readers so that they can relate to the understandings in a personal ways. This type of understanding is essentially completed through the crossing of oneself and others (Gadamer, 1989).

Interpretive Phenomenological Analysis (Smith, Flowers, & Larkin)

Interpretive phenomenological analysis (IPA) is a phenomenological psychology, which means that its aim is to study subjective experience. It is also an idiographic approach, meaning that its purpose is to show how people in given contexts make meaning of certain phenomena. IPA is theoretically grounded in hermeneutics, and its primary concepts stem from Edmund Husserl, Martin Heidegger, Jean-Paul Sartre, and Maurice Merleau-Ponty (Smith, Flowers, & Larkin, 2009). IPA is different from other phenomenological methods because of its use of idiographic approaches in combination with psychology and interpretation. In analysis, researchers identify their own preconceptions about the data and the attempts to suspend these (Husserl's concept of bracketing) so that they can focus on understanding the lived world of participants. As researchers analyze the data, they move back and forth between the transcribed experiences of participants and their own interpretation of what these experiences mean. Researchers also try to understand their participants' understanding of their own experiences, making this a double hermeneutic approach. In short, IPA is best suited to researchers who aim to understand an experience and how people with those experiences make sense of them.

Life-World Approach (Ashworth)

The life-world approach notes that the life-world has essential features and is universal to all human beings. Since classic phenomenological and existentialist authors never provided a thorough account of the phenomenology of the life-world (Ashworth, 2003a), Ashworth drew on points made by prominent philosophers such as Husserl, Heidegger, Boss, Merleau-Ponty, Sartre, and van den

Berg to construct essential features of the life-world in creating his approach. This essential structure of the life-world include seven sections: Selfhood (social identity, a person's sense of agency and how one feels about being present in a situation), Sociality (how a situation affects relationships with others), Embodiment (how a situation relates to feelings about one's body), Temporality (how sense of time is affected by a situation), Spatiality (how geography is affected by a situation), Project (how a situation relates to abilities to engage in important activities in one's life), and Discourse (terms used to describe the situation) (Ashworth, 2003). Researchers using the life-world approach try to recognize the world in perspectives of their participants. The life-world approach is considered a transformative approach where the view of the person is the same in a caring situation as it is in a learning situation (Ekebergh, 2009). Husserl's notion of reduction is used as researchers use bracketing to suspend presuppositions in order to reveal the life-world of participants. At each point, researchers reflect on narratives or participants' actions and attempt to discover what they observe or read says about the nature of the life-world of the participants while also being cognizant of their own propensities to trying to understand, using only perspectives that seem to accurately reflect the world of the participants (Ashworth & Ashworth, 2003).

Lived Experience Human Science Inquiry (van Manen)

Van Manen's reflective phenomenological method is aimed at illuminating the lived experience or prereflective experience of a phenomenon. In using this method, researchers depend on two concepts: reduction and vocative dimension. Using Husserl's concept of bracketing (reduction), researchers suspend their biases to understand the lived experience of a phenomenon. The aim of reduction in this method is to connect with the world directly and primitively (Merleau-Ponty, 1962) through experience rather than conceptualization. Emulating lived experiences happens through writing in this methodology, where researchers utilize the vocational dimension to create meaningful text recognized in prereflective experience (van Manen, 2017). The vocative dimension is a concept that a text can speak to a reader and the strength of a meaning is directly tied to the vocative nature of a text. Simply, the meaning of a text is stronger as it becomes more difficult to paraphrase or summarize the phenomenological interpretations. Max van Manen's method is grounded in many philosophers within the phenomenological tradition and is not exceedingly driven by specific techniques.

Reflective Life-World Approach (Dahlberg)

This approach is part of a tradition called caring science and is characterized by understanding people through a holistic approach. The holistic view requires seeing people in terms of their total situations (Dahlberg & Segesten, 2010). This method for reflective life-world work draws from the hermeneutic philosophies of Hans Gadamer and Paul Ricoeur, emphasizing that researchers must be curious about what they are studying and welcome surprise, as this is the only way that they will be able to move beyond their own interpretations and understand their participants' life-worlds. This approach is sometimes called the open life-world approach in that it is labeled an open method. Researchers are called to be patient, awaiting the phenomenon that reveals itself rather than depend on theories and models (Dahlberg, Dahlberg, & Nyström, 2008). To practice openness, researchers reflect on their own participation and contributions toward the object of study and how they relate to research participants. The reflective element of this life-world approach is an emphasis on bridling, which is a combination of Edmund Husserl's bracketing and Hans Gadamer's questioning. Bridling helps researchers shift their everyday reflections to scientific ones when they interrogate their assumptions and pre-understandings.

REFERENCES

Existential-Phenomenology

Fischer, W. F. (1985). Self-deception: An empirical-phenomenological inquiry into its essential meanings. In A. Giorgi (Ed.), *Phenomenology and psychological research* (pp. 118–154). Pittsburgh, PA: Duquesne University Press.

Giorgi, A. (1985). Sketch of a psychological phenomenological method. In A. Giorgi (Ed.), *Phenomenology and psychological research* (pp. 8–22). Pittsburgh, PA: Duquesne University Press.

Kierkegaard, S. (1988). *Stages on life's way.* Princeton, NJ: Princeton University Press.

Luijpen, W. A., & Koren, H. J. (1969). *A first introduction to existential phenomenology.* Pittsburgh, PA: Duquesne University Press.

von Eckartsberg, R. (1998a). Introducing existential-phenomenological psychology. In R. Valle (Ed.), *Phenomenological inquiry in psychology: Existential and transpersonal dimensions* (pp. 3–20). New York, NY: Plenum Press.

von Eckartsberg, R. (1998b). Existential-phenomenological research. In R. Valle (Ed.), *Phenomenological inquiry in psychology: Existential and transpersonal dimensions* (pp. 21–62). New York, NY: Plenum Press.

Warthhall, M. A. (2006). Existential phenomenology. In H. L. Dreyfus, & Wrathall, M. A. (Eds.), *A companion to phenomenology and existentialism* (pp. 229–239). Oxford, England: Blackwell.

Wertz, F. J. (1985). Method and findings in a phenomenological psychological study of a complex life event: Being criminally victimized. In A. Giorgi (Ed.), *Phenomenology and psychological research* (pp. 155–216). Pittsburgh, PA: Duquesne University Press.

Critical Narrative Analysis (Langdridge)

Gadamer, H. (2004) *Truth and method* (2nd rev. ed.). New York, NY: Continuum.

Langdridge, D. (2003). Hermeneutic phenomenology: Arguments for a new social psychology. *History and Philosophy of Psychology, 5*(1), 30–45.

Langdridge, D. (2004). The hermeneutic phenomenology of Paul Ricoeur: Problems and possibilities for existential–phenomenological psychotherapy. *Existential Analysis, 15*(2), 243–255.

Langdridge, D. (2007a). Gay affirmative therapy: A theoretical framework and defence. *Journal of Gay and Lesbian Psychotherapy, 11*(1/2), 27–43.

Langdridge, D. (2007b). *Phenomenological psychology: Theory, research and method.* Harlow, England: Pearson Education.

Langdridge, D. (2008). Phenomenology and critical social psychology: Directions and debates in theory and research. *Social and Personality Psychology Compass,* 2(3), 1126–1142.

Langdridge, D. (2009). Relating through difference: A critical narrative analysis. In L. Finlay & K. Evans (Eds.), *Relational centered research for psychotherapists: Exploring meanings and experience* (pp. 213–226). London, England: Wiley.

Ricoeur, P. (1970). *Freud and philosophy: An essay on interpretation.* (D. Savage, Trans.). New Haven, CT: Yale University Press.

Ricoeur, P. (1981). *Hermeneutics and the human sciences* (J. B. Thompson, Trans.). Paris, France: Edition de la Maison des Sciences de l'Homme/Cambridge, England: Cambridge University Press.

Ricoeur, P. (1996). *Lectures on ideology and utopia.* (G. H. Taylor, Ed.). New York, NY: Columbia University Press.

Dialogal Approach (Halling, Leifer, & Rowe)

Beck, B., Halling, S., McNabb, M., Miller, D., Rowe, J. O., & Schulz, J. (2003). Facing up to hopelessness: A dialogal phenomenological study. *Journal of Religion and Health,* 42(4), 339–354.

Halling, S., Kunz, G., & Rowe, J. O. (1994). The contributions of dialogal psychology to phenomenological research. *Journal of Humanistic Psychology,* 34(1), 109–131.

Halling, S., & Leifer, M (1991). The theory and practice of dialogal research. *Journal of Phenomenological Psychology,* 22, 1–15.

Halling, S., Leifer, M. & Rowe, J. O. (2006). Emergence of the dialogal approach: Forgiving another. In C. Fischer (Ed.), *Qualitative research methods for psychologists pp.* 247–277. Cambridge, MA: Academic Press.

Strasser, S. (1969). *The idea of dialogal phenomenology* (Duquesne studies, Philosophical series). Pittsburgh, PA: Duquesne University Press.

Dallas Approach (Garza)

Garza, G. (2004): Thematic moment analysis: A didactic application of a procedure for phenomenological analysis of narrative data. *Humanistic Psychologist, 32*(2), 120–168.

Garza. G. (2006). A clarification of Heidegger's phenomenology: A response to Kendler. *American Psychologist, 61*(3), 255–256.

Garza, G. (2007). Varieties of phenomenological research at the University of Dallas: An emerging typology. *Qualitative Research in Psychology, 4*(4), 313–342.

von Eckartsberg, R. (1998a). Introducing existential-phenomenological psychology. In R. Valle (Ed.), *Phenomenological inquiry in psychology: Existential and transpersonal dimensions* (pp. 3–20). New York, NY: Plenum Press.

Embodied Life-World Approach (Todres)

Gadamer, H. (1986). The relevance of the beautiful and other essays (R. Bernasconi, Ed.; N. Walker, Trans.). Cambridge, England: Cambridge University Press.

Gadamer, H. (1989) *Truth and method* (2nd ed.). London: Sheed & Ward.

Gadamer, H. (2004). *Truth and method* (2nd rev. ed.). New York, NY: Continuum.

Gendlin, E. T. (1973). Experiential phenomenology. In M. Natanson, *Phenomenology and the Social Sciences,* (pp. 281–319). Evanston, IL: Northwestern University Press.

Gendlin, E. T. (1978). Befindlichkeit: Heidegger and the philosophy of psychology. *Review of Existential Psychology and Psychiatry 16,* 1–3, 43–71.

Gendlin, E. T. (1981) *Focusing.* New York, NY: Bantam.

Gendlin, E. T. (1991) Language beyond patterns: Body, language, and situations. In B. den Outen & M. Moen, *The presence of feeling in thought* (pp. 22–151). New York, NY: Peter Lang.

Gendlin, E. T. (1996) *Focusing-oriented psychotherapy: A manual of the experiential method*. London, England: Guilford Press.

Gendlin, E. T. (2004) The new phenomenology of carrying forward. *Continental Philosophy Review 37*(1), 127–151.

Todres, L. (2007). *Embodied inquiry: Phenomenological touchstones for research, psychotherapy, and spirituality*. New York, NY: Palgrave Macmillan.

Todres, L. (2008). Being with that: The relevance of embodied understanding for practice. *Qualitative Health Research, 18*(11), 1566–1573.

Todres, L., & Galvin, K. T. (2008). Embodied interpretation: A novel way of evocatively re-presenting meanings in phenomenological research. *Qualitative Research, 8*(5), 568–583.

Interpretive Phenomenological Analysis (Smith, Flowers, & Larkin)

Reid, K., Flowers, P., & Larkin, M. (2005). Exploring lived experience. *The Psychologist, 18*, 20–23.

Shaw, R. L. (2001). Why use interpretative phenomenological analysis in health psychology? *Health Psychology Update, 10*, 48–52.

Smith, J. A. (1996). Beyond the divide between cognition and discourse: Using interpretative phenomenological analysis in health psychology. *Psychology & Health, 11*(2), 261–271.

Smith, J. A. (1999). Identity development during the transition to motherhood: An interpretative phenomenological analysis. *Journal of Reproductive and Infant Psychology, 17*(3), 281–299.

Smith, J. A. (2011). Evaluating the contribution of interpretative phenomenological analysis. *Health Psychology Review, 5*(1), 9–27.

Smith, J. A., Flowers, P., & Larkin, M. (2009). *Interpretative phenomenological analysis: Theory, method and research*. London, England: Sage.

Smith, J. A., Jarman, M., & Osborne, M. (1999). Doing interpretative phenomenological analysis. In M. Murray & K. Chamberlain (Eds.), *Qualitative Health Psychology* (pp. 218–240). London, England: Sage.

Smith, J. A., & Osborn, M. (2003) Interpretative phenomenological analysis. In J. A. Smith (Ed.), *Qualitative psychology: A practical guide to research methods.* London, England: Sage.

Smith, J. A., & Osborn, M. (2015). Interpretative phenomenological analysis as a useful methodology for research on the lived experience of pain. *British Journal of Pain, 9*(1), 41–42.

Life-World Approach (Ashworth)

Ashworth, A., & Ashworth, P. (2003). The lifeworld as phenomenon and as research heuristic, exemplified by a study of the lifeworld of a person suffering Alzheimer's disease. *Journal of Phenomenological Psychology, 34*(2), 179–205..

Ashworth, P. D. (1996). Presuppose nothing! The suspension of assumptions in phenomenological psychological methodology. *Journal of Phenomenological Psychology, 27,* 1–25.

Ashworth, P. D. (1997). The meaning of participation. *Journal of Phenomenological Psychology, 28,* 82–103.

Ashworth, P. D. (2003a). An approach to phenomenological psychology: The contingencies of the lifeworld. *Journal of Phenomenological Psychology, 34*(2), 145–156.

Ashworth, P. D. (2003b). The phenomenology of the lifeworld and social psychology. *Social Psychological Review, 5*(1), 18–34.

Ekebergh, M. (2009). Developing a didactic method that emphasizes lifeworld as a basis for learning. *Reflective Practice, 10*(1), 51–63.

Lived Experience Human Science Inquiry (van Manen)

Merleau-Ponty, M. (1962). *Phenomenology of perception.* New York, NY: Humanities Press.

van Manen, M. (1991). *The tact of teaching: The meaning of pedagogical thoughtfulness.* London, Ontario, Canada: Althouse Press.

van Manen, M. (1997). *Researching lived experience: Human science for an action sensitive pedagogy.* New York: State University of New York Press.

van Manen, M. (2007). Phenomenology & practice. *Phenomenology & Practice, 1*(1), 11–30.

van Manen, M. (2011). *Phenomenology online: A resource for phenomenological inquiry.* Retrieved from http://www.phenomenologyonline.com

van Manen, M. (2012). Ethics responsivity and pediatric parental pedagogy. *Phenomenology and Practice, 6*(1), 5–17.

Reflective Life-World Approach (Dahlberg)

Dahlberg, K. (2011). Lifeworld phenomenology for caring and for health care research. In G. Thomson, F. Dykes, & S. Downe (Eds.),. *Qualitative research in midwifery and childbirth: Phenomenological approaches* (pp. 17–34). London, England: Routledge.

Dahlberg, K., Dahlberg, H., & Nyström, M. (2008). *Reflective lifeworld research* (2nd ed.). Lund, Sweden: Studentlitteratur.

Dahlberg, K., & Ekebergh, M. (2008). To use a method without being ruled by it: Learning supported by drama in the integration of theory with healthcare practice. *The Indo-Pacific Journal of Phenomenology, 8,* 1–20.

Dahlberg, K., & Segesten, K. (2010). *Hälsa och vårdande* [Health and caring]. Stockholm, Sweden: Natur och Kultur.

Dahlberg, K., Todres, L., & Galvin, K. (2009). Lifeworld-led healthcare is more than patient-led care: An existential view of well-being. *Medicine Health Care and Philosophy, 12,* 265–271.

Creating Your Own Phenomenological Method

After reading Chapter 6, it is clear that many researchers have expanded on phenomenological concepts and methods to create research methodology that suited their purposes. Some created new methods based on other philosophers. Others borrowed from other disciplines to create new methods. Some combined various methods and philosophies in their construction of a new method. There are multiple reasons to create a new phenomenological method since phenomenology is such a personal process. Dissertation students who have never attempted phenomenological research or have not studied phenomenology are, of course, encouraged to start with Husserl or Heidegger before expanding out to other methods or creating their own. Learn the basics. In future studies, however, students who have become new scholars in the field and blooming phenomenological researchers can start to combine various phenomenological methods to create their own methodology. As researchers gain confidence and experience in using various phenomenological methods, individual methods can become more complex.

Perhaps a researcher wants to use interpretive phenomenological analysis (IPA) but does not agree with the concept of bracketing. In revising the method, a researcher can discuss Heidegger's concept of the hermeneutic circle and how it will be used to replace any kind of bracketing proposed in IPA method. The theoretical orientation would differ from the original method of IPA and some of the steps would change as the hermeneutic circle was utilized to manage biases and understandings. The most straightforward way to begin creating a new method is to combine different elements from different methods. In this chapter, a method created from two phenomenological methodologies is provided to demonstrate how to start the process of creating one's own phenomenological methodology. In this example, Amadeo Giorgi's existential-phenomenological method is supplemented with elements from Max van Manen's lived experience human science inquiry (four reflections) to create a new phenomenological method.

Giorgi's Five Basic Steps

1. Collection of verbal data
2. Reading of the data
3. Breaking of the data into some kind of parts
4. Organization and expression of the data from a disciplinary perspective
5. Synthesis or summary of the data for purposes of communication to the scholarly community.

van Manen's Four Reflections

A. **Corporeal Reflection**—Lived body or corporeality means that people are always bodily in the world.

B. **Spatial Reflection**—Lived space or spatiality is felt space or ways people experience space in daily existence.

C. **Temporal Reflection**—Lived time or temporality is participative time, how people experience time rather than time that is on the clock.

D. **Relational Reflection**—Lived other or communality and relationality are the lived relationships with others.

Illustrated Steps

(1) [GIORGI] Collecting of verbal data is done by interview within a semistructured process. The interview questions are open ended so that participants can express themselves extensively. During the interview, the researcher seeks to find a concrete and detailed description of each participant's experience as experienced by the participant.

(2) [GIORGI] Then the researcher reads the whole individual interview transcript of to get an initial sense of the participant's description. The goal is to acquire a global sense of the data to later determine how the parts are constituted.

(3) **[GIORGI]** After reading the entire transcript, the researcher breaks the elements into preliminary "meaning units" (Giorgi, 1985, p. 10), focusing on the topic being investigated. A meaning unit is the delineated portion of the data that is identified as a revealing characteristic of the phenomenon under investigation. The meaning unit is only a descriptive term, which means that the derived meaning will be clarified further. Additional data are obtained through follow-up individual interviews as needed. The researcher identifies any gaps in the data (missing information or unclear statements) given from the original transcript and formulates interview questions for each participant. The researcher interviews each participant for further description of each gap identified. The individual interview is transcribed, read over by the researcher, and integrated into the original analysis of meaning units.

(4) **[GIORGI]** Organization and expression of raw data into disciplinary language by redescribing them in psychological language so that the disciplinary value of each unit becomes more explicit. This creates a shift from perspectives language of everyday life to language within the psychological perspective used for analysis.

(5) **[GIORGI]** The rewritten meaning units are synthesized into a description of each participant's experience as an entire thematic description expressing the structure of the phenomenon The researcher creates a single description (structure or synthesis) for all of the participants in the study.

(6) **[VAN MANEN]** A reflection is written about the general description in Step 5, which further elucidates the meaning of the data as lived. The researcher uses corporeal (lived body), temporal (lived time), spatial (lived space), and relational (lived human relation) reflections (van Manen, 1997).

(7) **[GIORGI & VAN MANEN]** A general structure is written to provide a unification of all the major existential-phenomenological themes through lived experience.

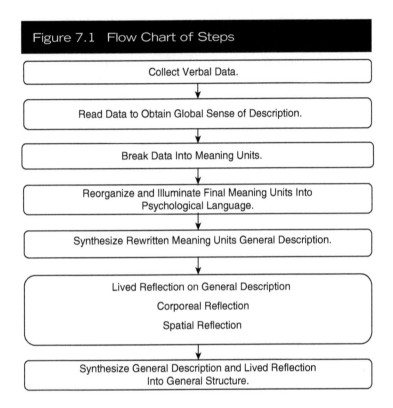

Figure 7.1 Flow Chart of Steps

Collect Verbal Data.

↓

Read Data to Obtain Global Sense of Description.

↓

Break Data Into Meaning Units.

↓

Reorganize and Illuminate Final Meaning Units Into Psychological Language.

↓

Synthesize Rewritten Meaning Units General Description.

↓

Lived Reflection on General Description

Corporeal Reflection

Spatial Reflection

↓

Synthesize General Description and Lived Reflection Into General Structure.

Results

The findings of this study begin with participants' demographics. A thematic cross-case analysis (Table 7.2) of the major themes that emerged is presented next; themes are ordered from most frequent occurrences to the least frequent. Final meaning units are expanded upon. Immediately following is the General Description of the evangelical Christian man who identifies as a sexual addict. A Reflection follows the General Description, providing a phenomenological thematic analysis through lived experience of the evangelical Christian man who identifies as a sexual addict. Finally, the General Structure provides a unification of all the key phenomenological themes in a unified description of the evangelical man who identifies as sexually addicted.

Participant Demographics

The data that were collected were from participants who were evangelical Christian men identifying as sexual addicts and who stated that they were in recovery from their addictions. Individual interviews were 1 hour in duration, and follow-up interviews lasted 30 minutes on average. All participants were married and identified as heterosexual males, though one participant stated that he engaged in homosexual activities in the past. The participants provided their ages, marital statuses, durations of marriages, durations of time they identified as evangelical Christians, and durations of time in sexual sobriety (Table 7.1).

The next table (Table 7.2) shows the themes that emerged in this research study with themes organized in an order of most frequent themes to least frequent themes.

Table 7.1 Participants' Demographic Data

Participant	Age	Years Married	Years Being Evangelical	Years Sexual Sobriety
P1	47	25	30	4.5
P2	39	20	17	3.5
P3	47	20	27	1.5
P4	49	23	40	5
P5	70	28	28	28
P6	69	42	5	4.5

Table 7.2 Thematic Cross-Case Analysis

Theme	P1	P2	P3	P4	P5	P6
Conflicted Childhood	X	X	X	X	X	X
Disconnection From Father or Mother	X	X	X	X	X	X

(Continued)

Table 7.2 (Continued)

Theme	P1	P2	P3	P4	P5	P6
Initial Sexual Exploration and Action	X	X	X	X	X	X
Married Life Separated From Sexual Life	X	X	X	X	X	X
Religious Life Separated From Sexual Life	X	X	X	X	X	X
Reaction Formation Parallel	X	X	X	X	X	X
Religious Guilt Over Sexual Behaviors	X	X	X	X	X	X
Marital Guilt Over Sexual Behaviors	X	X	X	X	X	X
Coping by Using Sexuality or Fantasy	X	X	X	X	X	X
Depending on God/ Program Daily	X	X	X	X	X	X
Creating a Marital Hierarchy	X	X	X	X		X
Continued Struggles in Marriage	X	X	X	X		X
Seeing Marriage as Solution to Sexual Problems	X	X	X		X	X
Affirmation Through Sex or Illicit Relationships	X	X		X	X	X
Rationalizing Through God	X		X	X	X	X
Asking God to Change Him	X	X	X	X	X	
Unrealistic Expectations About Sex	X		X	X		X

Theme	P1	P2	P3	P4	P5	P6
Initial Trouble in Marriage	X	X	X	X		
Preoccupation With Sexual Behavior	X		X	X		X
Messages From God	X	X	X		X	
Blaming Spouse	X		X	X		
Confusion Over Spiritual Leadership	X	X	X			
Sexual Addiction as God's Will	X		X	X		
Church Unhelpful		X	X			
Angry at God			X	X		

General Description

. . . .

The General Description of the sexually addicted evangelical Christian man emerged from the final meaning units through integration of themes into a general description of participants' experiences of struggling with sexual addiction as evangelical Christian men. The General Description conserves and incorporates all of the participants' accounts while organizing data within the psychological discipline and highlighting experiential meanings.

All of the participants had family conflict that they experienced as emotional abuse and other traumas of various degrees. They experience disconnectedness with either their mothers or fathers, mostly fathers. It was due to counseling and support groups that participants were able to realize that their parental disconnections made an impact on their unfavorable sexual behaviors as adults. While they were sexually acting out, participants felt inadequate, and most of them used sex as a way to feel better and affirm their masculinity. All of the participants sexually explored as they grew up in childhood and adolescence, yet none of them discussed sexuality with their parents. Throughout their childhood and adolescent sexual explorations, participants felt guilt and shame because they thought it was sinful. Most of the participants felt guilty because of sexual behaviors like masturbation or sex out of wedlock. Despite the guilt, they continued to engage in illicit sexual behaviors because the guilt would come after a sexual act they thought was sinful. While guilt was ever-present throughout their sexual exploration phases, it did not feel oppressive.

Most of the participants felt conflict between their sexual exploring and their religious beliefs. They believed that marriage would solve their sexual problems and that they would stop acting out sexually after they were married to women because their wives would grant them their sexual desires and fill their sexual needs. Expectations from marriage ranged from thinking sex would always be available to them with a willing partner who would match their sexual desires to fantasy-type sexual expectations borrowed from media and pornography.

Early in their marriages, problems began with spouses that ranged from conflict in personality to unwanted pregnancies. Marital problems increased for participants as responsibilities increased through having children, needing money, and medical issues. Spiritual leadership was a concept that some participants felt confusion about because they did not know what God expected of them as spiritual leader or how they should behave in that role. While not all of the participants experienced conflict over spiritual leadership roles, most believed that they should be the leaders in their marriages and households.

Since many participants either did not know how to be spiritual leaders or knew they were not leading their families spiritually as God would intend, they felt discontent from their wives, who expected them to lead spiritually. Stress continued to increase in their marriages over spiritual leadership, and so participants coped by sexually acting out in illicit ways. Sexual behaviors differed from engaging with strippers to watching pornography to engaging in illicit romantic relationships with other women. Some men would plan their schedules to correlate with their sexual behaviors in a way that their behaviors became just as important as other responsibilities in their lives. Many of these men traveled, and travel helped them feel free to sexually act out. Other men used time away at work or waited until their wives were sleeping or away to engage in sexual behaviors.

All of these men felt guilt over their illicit sexual acts. Some did not feel that they were hurting anyone else if they engaged in sexual acts like viewing pornography rather than engaging with another woman in a sexual way, but this changed for all of them as they progressed in their sexually addictive behaviors. Many would blame their wives for their sexual behaviors because they felt that their wives were not meeting their sexual or emotional needs. Some would be angry with God about their situations, but most did not view God negatively. Almost all of the men begged God to change them and release them of their sexual desires. When their sexual desires continued, they dealt with unanswered prayers by either escaping responsibility through rationalizations to depending on God's forgiveness after engaging in an illicit sexual act. Some even felt so overwhelmed by their guilt that illicit sexual behaviors were their direct coping mechanisms. Hence, others subjected their eternal souls to hell because of their inability to stop sexually acting out and rationalized that they should just do whatever they wanted in this life. All of these men separated their married lives from their illicit sexual lives and would lie to their spouses when they were asked about suspicious behaviors. In marriage counseling, for those who attended, none volunteered information about their sexual behaviors despite trying to work on their marriages at the time of engaging in illicit sexual behaviors. The separation of married life and illicit sexual life progressed naturally for all participants.

The religious lives of participants were also separated from their illicit sexual lives. To friends from church, they put up a façade of perfection. They pretended to be loyal husbands, dedicated fathers, and loyal church members. They were all heavily involved in church during the time they were engaging in sexually illicit acts. Most were leaders in their churches—elders, deacons, Sunday school pastors, and congregation speakers. Church involvement and leadership in their churches gave many participants a form of self-validation while others felt conflict over their roles. As these men continually persisted in the separating their religious and marital lives from their illicit sexual lives, they felt guilty and fearful. Most did not divulge any information about their sexual behaviors until they were forced by big consequences. While some of the participants sought help from the leaders in their churches, they did not think the guidance received to be helpful and continued to sexually act out.

All of these men took steps to change after they were either exposed or confronted with consequences. It was in these consequences that participants experienced God's divine intervention. They were only then moved to admit to what they had been doing and seek help in recovery. All of them heavily relied on God through a recovery program to help them. However, their marriages experienced significant stress even years after recovery work, mostly in the areas of trust. Most of these men took on personal responsibility and worked toward becoming spiritual leaders in the way that they felt God intended. During this time, power struggles ensued within some marriages as men tried to reestablish leadership roles. All participants looked on their sexual struggles as either lessons from God or God's will for their lives to become spiritual men.

Reflection

The Reflection is a thematized lived-experience account of the evangelical Christian man who believes he is sexually addicted by way of Max van Manen's (1997) four reflections: corporeal reflection (lived body), temporal reflection (lived time), spatial reflection (lived space), and relational reflection (lived human relation).

Corporeal Reflection (Lived Body)

In many points throughout the lives of these men, they experienced conflict between their bodies and religious faith. While being aroused in a sexual ways felt physically pleasurable, it was also distressing because of their religious beliefs. These men were continually pulled between a desire for sexual exploration and a desire to be sexually moral. As they became adults, a separation ensued between carnal pleasures and religious convictions. Both elements opposed one another quite strongly, so these men felt conflict in both spaces as they engaged in immoral sexual acts or moral religious activities. Whey they were young children and adolescents, guilt was a constant theme in their lives. P1, P2, and P4 felt guilty about their masturbation while in college, while P1 hid the notion that he masturbated from any of his friends because he thought it was a sin despite finding it difficult to stop. P3 felt guilt over sexual arousal at any time due to his religious beliefs and when he viewed and masturbated to pornography. While P5 and P6 stated they did not feel guilty over engaging in sexual exploration in their childhoods or as adolescents, they noted that they did not feel that they were fully dedicated to God or their religion at those points in their lives. When P5 increased his involvement in evangelical religion, guilt emerged when he looked at pornography or attended peep shows. P6 stated that he became serious about evangelical faith right before his sexual recovery work despite being actively involved in his church through all of his life.

Temporal Reflection (Lived Time)

Engagement with others in adulthood was greatly shaped by childhood experiences. P1 experienced feelings of inadequacy as his father's son when he was young, and this learned inadequacy forced him to validate himself as a man through sexual means with other women and self-stimulation. He felt that a woman who was right for him would eventually validate his manhood and take all of his feelings of childhood inadequacy away from his adult mind. P2 felt abandoned and inadequate as a boy when his father left, and these feelings continued in adulthood. Through sexual liaisons with other women and a guise of perfection, he aimed to validate himself as a man and cope with feelings of inadequacy. Because P3's mother abused him emotionally and told him about his father's irresponsibility and heavy pornography use, P3 copied his father's ways. He viewed pornography online quite profoundly and refused to be responsible for family decisions. He depended on his spouse to lead the family and make all the decisions. He became his father, and his wife resented the same traits of character in him that his mother resented in his father: irresponsibility and a dependence on pornography. Because P4 always felt unloved, not safe, and inadequate when he was growing up, those feelings followed him in adulthood. To cope, he sexually engaged with numerous partners to feel loved and to feel safe. He had trouble letting go of his illicit sexual affairs and tried to hold on to them for as long as possible, even proposing marriage to some. P5 experienced disconnection from his mother because he felt that she did not want to take the time to talk with him when he needed her. He felt unworthy and inadequate as a child because of his relationship with his mother, and these feelings translated to his relationship with his wife. When his wife was upset with him or if he felt she was dissatisfied, he would immediately feel inadequate and cope with those feelings of inadequacy by engaging in illicit sex acts. P6 felt that he was an outcast and a scapegoat in his family. He had two overachieving brothers, and he felt like an underachiever in relation to them. He was convinced his parents viewed him as an underachiever, and as his feelings of inadequacy continued into adulthood, he took refuge in being a master seducer. His over-achievement in his ability to seduce women and the envy other men felt for his skills helped P6 feel good about himself.

All of these men viewed their sexual addictions as avenues that allowed them to grow closer in their relationships with God. They believed they became better spiritual men. Those struggles of the past were blessings in their present because they grew closer to God than ever before.

Spatial Reflection (Lived Space)

All of the men developed spaces that hosted their separate lives, sexual, spiritual, and marital. When some of the participants traveled or had some time that was separate from their church lives and marital lives, they were free to engage in illicit sexual activities without having to face the morals of their religious beliefs. P1 scheduled his travel time to correlate with his affair partners' free times. P2 would sexually engage with women at work and with women in the area of where he was away for military work. P3 planned his pornography watching around the absence of his wife and their child. P4 lied to his wife about being at work while he sexually engaged with other women. P5 went to strip clubs and sexual massage parlors while he used his work schedule as an excuse for his absence from his home, and P6 sexually engaged with various women at work. Within their separated worlds, some men felt guilt and shame because of their behaviors, thoughts, and feelings, but all continued to sexually act out regardless of those feelings of guilt and shame. Because they separated their worlds, they were able to better hide the actions they knew to be sexu-ally immoral from their families and their church relationships. As stress built in one world, each man used the other two worlds to cope and alleviate stressors. If married life got to be too over-whelming, the men would sexually act out in their sexual-worlds to alleviate stress. When any one world got to be too emotionally overwhelming for them, they had two other worlds to help them escape. Since all of them served in leadership roles in their church lives, they felt a sense of morality during their leadership activities, which alleviated much of the immediate emotional stress, guilt, and shame they were feeling at that moment. While those feelings never stopped, these men were able to run from them as they moved from one world to the next. Once they started feeling guilt and shame as they stayed in church leadership roles, at times feeling like hypocrites, they escaped to their sexual-worlds for immediate physical gratification to cope once again. Eventually, the three worlds converged because many of the men were exposed or feared exposure and because consequences got to be too big for all of the men to face. This is when change happened, and only then did all of the men combine their three worlds into one, with much revision, of course. Since the sexual-world did not fit with the balance of married life and church life, the sexual-worlds had to be revised to start to develop healthy and moral sexual unions in their marriages. Full confessions to spouses inevitably followed, apart from P6, who kept many of his past affairs secret.

Relational Reflection (Lived Human Relation)

Conflicted childhoods were backgrounds that all of the participants had in common. P5 was not as explicit as the other participants about his childhood struggles, but as he spoke throughout the interview, he presented a clear story of conflict in his childhood upbringing. For example, when he spoke about the relationship he had with his dad, he was weepy, and when he discussed engagements with this mother, he was consistently ambivalent about his relationship with her. As meaning units were analyzed, P5's childhood showed a strict household with a mother that was distant and with a low emotional connection to either parent. All of the other participants grew up with fathers who were absent from them either emotionally, physically, or both. P1 and P2 felt the emptiness in their lives due to the limited relationships they had with their fathers, and P3 and P4 were both angry at their dads' absence and the way they acted when they were present. P6 was not explicit about how he felt toward his parents, but he rather stated that he felt like an outcast and that his parents looked down on him in many ways.

All of the men except one thought that marriage would heal them from sexual desires they deemed deviant and their illicit sexual behaviors. In fact, they pictured their wives in certain ways before they ever met them, projecting expectations on them that allowed them to look forward to relief from sin after marriage. Marriage was the answer to all of their deviant problems. Many thought that they would be able to have sex whenever and however they wanted after they were married so they did not have to look for sexual gratifications elsewhere. To them, sex in marriage would be more exciting and more frequent. They no longer had to struggle with immoral sexual desires. P1 prayed to God for a wife who would alleviate his immoral sexual behaviors and his urges. He imagined sex with his wife would be just like the couples he viewed through pornography. P2 thought marriage would help him feel sexually adequate and that he would no longer feel the need to conquer other women to help himself feel secure. Hence, marriage neither filled those needs nor solved those problems, and both men were resentful toward their wives. P3 and P4 thought that marriage was the answer to sexual needs and that their wives would fill all of their sexual desires. Hence, these two were both disappointed, as the sex in their marriages was not as frequent as expected, so both engaged in illicit sexual acts to fill the sexual voids they felt. P6 believed he would stop masturbating to pornography after he was married, but when he still had a deep desire to view pornography and masturbate after he was married to his wife, he let his illicit sexual behaviors continue while hiding his pornography use from his wife. The consequence of P6's heavy pornography use was boredom in his marriage. He had so much variety from pornographic images and story lines that he thought of his sexual relationship with his wife to be mundane, and he eventually started having affairs with other women to fill increased sexual desires created from pornography use. P5 was married twice, and both times, when sex decreased with each wife, he increased his illicit sexual behaviors to fill the sexual voids he felt instead of working on his marital relationships. He would engage sexually with women in massage parlors, frequent strip clubs, and engage with women in sex shops.

Early problems in marriage were patterns for all the men, and those problems became bigger when more responsibilities or life challenges were introduced, such as children, illnesses, or work issues. To cope, all of the participants engaged in sexually illicit behaviors to escape their problems for moments in time. As the problems were not addressed appropriately in their marriages, problems grew bigger, and new problems arose from the neglect. Stress inevitably increased among many marital and familiar responsibilities, and participants found themselves overwhelmed and emotionally moved further away from their wives. They coped with illicit sexual behaviors such as fantasizing an escape (P1), prolonged extramarital affairs (P2, P6), masturbation and pornography use (P3, P4), and having sex with other women (P5, P6).

Most of these men felt worth when they engaged in illicit sexual acts. P1 felt abandoned by his friend when he was in college, and he masturbated more to cope. P2 felt good about his manhood with every woman he sexually conquered. He felt pride in his talent to seduce women who were beautiful and when his male friends were envious of him. When he was a child, P4 masturbated to pornography because he felt unloved and insecure due to the dynamics of his family upbringing. P5 felt instantly better at strip clubs because dancers were stripping for him, and his feelings of being a failed husband temporarily disappeared.

Through the years of illicit sexual escapes, these men's wives grew angry because their husbands grew more irresponsible and distant from them. Spiritual leadership was an expectation that they had, and they realized how obviously their husbands were failing at this Godly expectation. It was a big point of contention in the marriage. Though God is not a human being, evangelical Christians have a relationship with God that is personal and is primary to their beliefs. Therefore, relationships that participants have with God is discussed in this relational reflection. All participants except P6 depended on God to change their sexual ways and to free them of illicit sexual desires. In recovery, P5 continues to depend on God to help him avoid acting on sexual urges that are immoral and vows that God is helping as he prays and continuously asks God for guidance. In the past, when God did not take away the sexual urges of P1 and P2 despite their prayers, they grew angry with Him. Interestingly enough, all of these men used their relationships with God to continue to sexually act out. While P1 continued illicit sexual acts under the assumption that he was going to go to hell anyway, P2 blamed God's unwillingness to take away his sexual desires as evidence of powerlessness and the need to bend to temptation. After he engaged in illicit sexual acts, he immediately asked for God's forgiveness, promising he would do better next time. Hence, his cycle continued. P3, P5, and P6 also depended on the forgiveness of God to feel cleansed after sexually acting out. P4's feelings of powerlessness and overwhelming guilt over his sexual indiscretions and sinning against God were his excuse to momentarily stop feeling so bad about sinning and sin some more through illicit sex. With each illicit sexual act, his shame about wronging God would increase, and he escaped those negative feelings with more illicit sexual acts.

In recovery, all of the men understood their relationships with God in ways that differed from their understandings during their sexually addictive lifestyles. P1 let go of his high expectations about who he thought he should be as a Godly man. Expectations from the literal Biblical interpretations were exchanged for a dependence on God's mercy and doing the best that he could as an imperfect and inherently sinful man. P2 started to incorporate God in the bedroom with his wife through revering God as he bonded with his wife through sex. He stated that he appreciated his wife more and depended on his adoration of God to bond with his wife in the marriage bed. He did not view sex as just physical anymore but as a way to become more emotionally tied to his wife and to God. P3 and P4 deemed their sexual addictions as parts of God's plans for their lives to deepen their dependence on Him, which was something they felt grateful about. P5 and P6 depended on God to help them avoid acting on sexual temptations rather than acting out now and asking for God's forgiveness later. P5 still struggled with fully depending on God to help him avoid temptation and wrestled with the dependence he had on personal willpower.

All of the men grew more dependent on God and closer to Him as they continued to work on themselves in their recovery programs. Despite still struggling with problems in their marriages, God was now their greatest source of help, though P5 still stated that he had some power to give to God and that he depended on himself much of the time to stay in recovery. All of these men's relationships with God were necessary to their marital successes. God was now the primary entity to help them solve problems in their marriages. Participants, along with their spouses, prayed for guidance and change when difficult situations arose. P1 and P3 were married to women who were not evangelical, so these two participants spoke of a separate personal relationship with God instead of a triadic one (i.e., God, husband, and wife). Hence both of them would continually strive to include God in their marriages and talk about Him as the third entity between husband and wife. For all of these men, God was absolutely necessary to help them be loyal husbands and good fathers.

General Structure

The General Structure is a presentation of the existential-phenomenological themes implicit in all the participants' experiential narratives. It is a divergence from individual viewpoints and experiences of participants. The unification of the main existential-phenomenological themes are presented in a cohesive summary to illustrate the lived experience of the evangelical Christian man who identifies himself as a sexual addict.

The evangelical man who identifies as sexually addicted lives his life through three compartmentalized worlds (religious, marital, and sexual). In the beginning, there is a regimented understanding of the expression of sexual desires within a religious moral code. This clash of sexual desires and religious morality creates a phase of sexual explorations that is fraught with conflict. To cope with sexual desires and religious expectations of remaining sexually pure, evangelical men compartmentalize their personal worlds into different areas of their lives that they move among as they desire, but they are always met with conflict within each world. When they want to engage in sexual exploration, religious moral codes remind them of their sinful ways and discourage those engagements. Hence sexual urges most often overcome religious morals, and sexual behaviors are acted upon. Shortly after, guilt and shame overwhelm these men, and the sexual pleasure they recently felt is muted and becomes a great source of shame and guilt. However, when they sexually act out, the physical pleasures they feel in those moments give them emotional relief from conflicts they experienced in their childhoods and move them away from their feelings of inadequacy, at least in the moment. Patterns of sexual relief, coping, and feelings of shame and guilt continue into predictable patterns for them, constituting a greater psychological separation of sexual-world and religious-world. Religious beliefs are used to rationalize engaging in illicit sexual acts due to either being angry with God for failing to deliver them from sexual temptation or hopelessness over being sinners doomed to hell in the afterlife. Asking for God's forgiveness after illicit sexual engagements becomes a dependence, and looking forward to marriage to save them from sexual desires and immoral behaviors is now the focus as men realize God's lack of deliverance from sexual temptations in their current lives. When their wives fail to deliver them from sexual temptations and engaging in illicit sexual acts, a third world is created to separate the marital life from the unsaved illicit sexual life. The spiritual space stays separate as wives' disapproving attitudes about their husbands' spiritual leadership do not fit into the spiritual facades that they created in their church environments as spiritual leaders.

As illicit sexual acts continue and sexual immorality remains in conflict with marriage and religious beliefs, these evangelical men cope with moral and value conflicts by meeting their immediate needs within each separate world to escape stressors from the other worlds. If men feel overwhelmingly guilty about engaging in sexually illicit behaviors in their sexual-worlds when they enter the marriage-world and face their partners, for example, their spiritual-worlds offer them relief in their leadership roles as their church congregants revere them as decent and moral men. Every compartmentalized world relieves negative feelings from the other two worlds and is inherently separate because of the conflict one has with the other. The worlds are incongruent and in their current states, unable to unify. While the religious-world expects moral men who spiritually lead their families, the marital space recognizes the failure of these men's spiritual leadership skills. While the marital-world is fraught with the most conflict, the sexual-world provides these men with the most immediate relief while adding more guilt and shame as a consequence.

These compartmentalized life-worlds cannot be unified in their current states, and hiding their existence is necessary to create an acceptable façade to people in each separate world. All men stay silent about their situations, rarely reaching out for guidance or help from others. Shame and guilt rule most of these men's behaviors, and they live in a lonely and misunderstood world no matter which life-world they find themselves in because they are continuously misunderstood by others (a consequence of their own doing). Eventually, growing consequences propel these men to face the reality of their problems and address their behaviors honestly, through confrontation and guidance from God. This forced surrender to change suspends the illicit sexual-world while men work to harmonize their religious- and marital-worlds. Sexuality comes later through recovery, dedication to their marriages, and working on earning trust from their spouses (which is the challenge that is most difficult for them).

The label of *sexual addict* is something that provides these men with relief as they join with other men in the evangelical community who also identify as sexual addicts. No longer do they feel that they are bad men. They are now men with an illness and men who are not alone as they identify with others in their recovery programs who have experienced similar struggles and provide them with hope that things can improve with God's help. Their increased reliance on their relationship with God and the guidance they receive in their recovery programs give them a renewed appreciation and respect for God.

As emerging scholars grow more and more confident, many twists and turns can emerge in creating a phenomenological method that suits the researcher. This is completely acceptable. To stay rigidly within one method that may not suit a researcher in its entirety is never encouraged. Phenomenology itself consists of various orientations, and many schools of phenomenology contradict one another because phenomenology is such a personal discipline. Phenomenological inquiry draws on all kinds of sources to discover meanings, and many of those sources are not within the social sciences. Poetry, daily life, theology, and art are just some sources for illuminating meaning in phenomenological inquiry. By its very nature, phenomenology is an ever-changing tradition. Researchers who want to continue to research topics through phenomenological methods are encouraged to take an eclectic approach. Learning and applying the "basics" (i.e., Husserl and Heidegger) is just the beginning of the journey.

REFERENCES AND RESOURCES

Edger, K. (2009). Evangelical Christian men who identify as sexual addicts: An existential-phenomenological investigation. *Sexual Addiction and Compulsivity, 16*, 289–323.

Edger, K. (2011). *Losing the bond with God: Sexual addiction and evangelical men*, Santa Barbara, CA: Praeger.

Giorgi, A. (1985). Sketch of a psychological phenomenological method. In A. Giorgi, *Phenomenology and psychological research* (pp. 8–22). Pittsburgh, PA: Duquesne University Press.

Giorgi, A. (1997). The theory, practice, and evaluation of the phe-nomenological method as a qualitative research procedure. *Journal of Phenomenological Psychology, 28,* 235–260.

van Manen, M. (1997). *Researching lived experience: Human science for an action sensitive pedagogy.* New York: State University of New York Press.

van Manen, M. (2007). Phenomenology & practice. *Phenomenology & Practice, 1*(1), 11–30.

van Manen, M. (2011). *Phenomenology online: A resource for phenom-enological inquiry.* Retrieved from http://www.phenomenologyonline .com

Appendix A

..

Recruitment Flyer

Name of your University

An Investigation of the Lived Experiences of Evangelical Christian Men Who Self-Identify as Sexual Addicts

VOLUNTEERS WANTED FOR A RESEARCH STUDY

You are being invited to participate in a research study that seeks to investigate the lived experience of evangelical Christian men who self-identify as sexual addicts. You will be asked to participate in one focus group with several other men (approximately 90 minutes) and participate in a follow-up individual interview (approximately 60 minutes). The topic of both interviews is your experiences of being an evangelical male who self-identifies as a sexual addict. The interviews will be videotaped and/or audiotaped.

In order to participate you must meet the following criteria:

1) Must be at least 18 years of age.
2) Must identify as an evangelical Christian.
3) Must identify as a sexual addict.

Your Confidentiality

This study is not affiliated with any group, and no one will know you are participating, other than the researcher and other participants in the focus group. Reporting of the results will not include any identifiers. All personal identifiers will be removed by the researcher, and all audio and video tapes will be destroyed immediately after the study.

If you are interested in participating in this study or would like more information, please contact:

[Your Name] at: 999-999-9999 or youremailhere@gmail.com

All communication is confidential.

Appendix B

Screening

PARTICIPANTS MUST

1) be 18 years of age or older.

2) meet the criteria for evangelical Christians.

3) self-identify as recovering sexual addicts.

4) use the same language as the researcher (English).

THE CRITERIA FOR QUALIFYING AS AN EVANGELICAL CHRISTIAN ARE BELIEFS IN

1) the absolute authority of biblical scripture as a source of knowledge of God and how to live a Christian life;

2) Jesus Christ as God incarnate and the savior of sinful humankind;

3) the lordship of the Holy Spirit;

4) the necessity of personal conversion (being born again);

5) the need to evangelize both individually and as a church;

6) the importance of the communion of Christians for spiritual sustenance, fellowship, and development.

Appendix C

Semi-Structured Interview Guide

After a brief introduction about the focal point of the research, the focus group (or subjects) will be asked to describe their lived experiences as if to someone who had never heard of sexually addicted relationships.

The queries that frame the discussion will be the following:

1) Describe your sexual addiction.
2) Has your religion had an impact on your sexual addiction?
3) **If not,** discuss how your religion has remained separate from your sexual addiction.
4) **If so,** give an example of a time where your religion had an impact on your sexual addiction.
5) Has your religion had an impact on your views about sexuality?
6) **If not,** give examples of how your religion remained separate from your views about sexuality.
7) **If so,** give an example of a time where your religion had a helpful impact on your views about sexuality.
8) **If so,** give an example of a time where your religion had a harmful impact on your views about sexuality.

Appendix D

· ·

Consent to Participate

Name of your University

Street Address ◆ *City, State Zip Code*

CONSENT TO PARTICIPATE IN A RESEARCH STUDY

TITLE: The Lived Experience of
                               Evangelical Christian Men
                               Who Self-Identify as Sexual
                               Addicts

INVESTIGATOR: Your Name

                               Street Address

                               City, State Zip Code

                               999-999-9999

ADVISOR: (if applicable:) Name of your chair and
                               credentials

                               Your University

                               Your School (ex: School of
                               Behavioral Health)

                               Your Department (ex: Dept. of
                               Counselor Education)

SOURCE OF SUPPORT:	This study is being performed as partial fulfillment of the requirements for the doctoral degree in counselor education and supervision at _____ University.
PURPOSE:	You are being asked to participate in a research project that seeks to investigate the lived experience of evangelical Christian men who self-identify as sexual addicts. You will be asked to participate in a focus group interview and a follow-up individual interview. Your lived experiences of being an evangelical male who self-identifies as sexually addicted will be the topic. The interviews will be audio and videotaped and transcribed. The group interview will last approximately 90–120 minutes, and the individual interview will last approximately 60 minutes. If you choose not to participate in the focus group interview for any reason, you may participate in an individual interview with the researcher (approximately 90 minutes) and a follow-up individual interview (approximately 60 minutes); both will be tape-recorded. These are the only requests that will be made of you.

RISKS AND BENEFITS: The risks may include emotional discomfort created from discussing your sexual addiction. A risk may exist that confidential information may be disclosed by other group members in the focus group. Other risks involved are no greater than those encountered in everyday life. This study is not affiliated with any group, and no one will know you are participating other than the researcher and other participants in the focus group.

COMPENSATION: Participants will not be compensated in any way. However, participation in the project will require no monetary cost to you.

CONFIDENTIALITY: All research materials (written and taped) will be stored in a locked file in the researcher's home. The videotaped and audiotaped discussion parts of the session will be transcribed, and I will remove all identifying material about you and any others that you talk about. Final data that is reported will be drawn from the transcriptions without identifiers. Audiotapes and videotapes will be destroyed immediately after they are transcribed; all other research materials will be kept for a period of no more than 5 years following the completion of research. The information in this research study will be held confidential by the researcher, although due to the participation in a focus group, the researcher cannot guarantee that subjects' information will remain confidential among its group members.

RIGHT TO WITHDRAW: You are under no obligation to participate in this study. You are free to withdraw at any time.

SUMMARY OF RESULTS: A summary of the results of this research will be supplied to you, at no cost, upon request.

VOLUNTARY CONSENT: I have read the above statements and understand what is being requested of me. I also understand that my participation is voluntary and that I am free to withdraw my consent at any time, for any reason. On these terms, I certify that I am willing to participate in this research project.

I understand that should I have any further questions about my participation in this study, I may call [Your Name] at 999-999-9999 or by e-mail at youremailhere@gmail.com, Dr. Dissertation Chair (your chair) at 999-999-9999 or by e-mail at yourchairemailhere@university.edu, or Dr. IRB, Chair of the _____ University Institutional Review Board, at 999-999-9999.

_____   _____

Participant's Signature   Date

_____   _____

Researcher's Signature   Date

Appendix E

Sample Dissertation Literature Review

Source

Little, M. K. (n.d.). *Living with chronic illnesses: How are those with a chronic illness treated by their families since their diagnosis?* Retrieved from https://libguides.uwf.edu/c.php? g=215199&p=1420828

Literature Review

Chronic physical illness and chronic mental illnesses are reviewed separately here due to the tremendous differences in the two. In this study, they will be compared against one another to cross-analyze the differences and similarities in how the family member is treated depending upon the type of illness the family member has.

Chronic Physical Illness

Chronic physical illnesses vary in types and intensity, but have one characteristic in common: They recur throughout time, usually at random intervals. The uncertainty that comes along with a diagnosis along these lines can greatly affect family communication and relationships.

Marriage. Marriage is the basis of most families in many cultures. Keeping the marital bond strong could be very difficult in the face of a chronic physical illness. A chronic physical illness could potentially change the daily lives and interactions of the entire marital relationship. It is important to discuss the communication that occurs around theses illnesses in order to understand how those who have one have been treated since their diagnosis based on research already conducted around similar communication processes. Badr and Acitelli (2005) found that in couples who used relationship talk, or talking about the nature and direction of the relationship, chronically ill couples had more benefit than a couple who did not include someone who had a chronic physical illness. This literature proves that in a situation where a spouse is chronically ill, it is important to use communication to make one another aware of certain things such as how one felt about a situation, or what one needs or expects from their partners. Talking about the state of the relationship can be helpful for chronically ill people to express fears in relation to their illness and the marriage. Berg and Upchurch (2007) suggested that collaborative talk is the type of communication that is commonly correlated with positive results. This shows that it is important for married couples to talk about their situation together to keep their relationship strong since these tactics have been proven to be helpful for the couple. Shuff and Sims (2013) add to this by stating that couples that are aware of their partner's expectations of communication in the marriage are more successful in supporting one another. Being aware of the partner's desires and being able to fill them is central to satisfaction in the relationships' functioning. Marital coping and sharing is not limited to relationship talk, though. Another powerful way of sharing within the family is through narrative.

Narratives. Something that is strongly recognized and praised throughout literature on chronic physical illnesses is narrative. Several studies (Freeman & Couchonnal, 2006; Ott Anderson & Geist Martin, 2003; Walker & Dickson, 2004) stress the importance of narratives for the family healing process. Narratives are beneficial because they allow research to capture personal accounts of illness and let the ill persons be gatekeepers to their own information about their illness. Ott Anderson and Geist Martin (2003) state that those with a chronic physical illness are more likely to actively share if their feelings and perceptions are confirmed by other people, especially friends and family. Some chronic illnesses have a negative social stigma to them, and confirmation that people will be respectful is important to getting patients to open up about their experiences. Narratives and storytelling help families to communicate about changes that have taken place. Ott Anderson and Geist Martin (2003) conclude that the ever-changing identity in the face of illness never stops; it is an endless development. Sharing through narrative in cases of chronic physical illness has the potential to better family communication because the patient is able to clearly and concisely explain what is happening to him or her from a personal point of view. This can help the family identify what the patient has gone through, as well as understand new emerging identities. However, Lorde (1980) points out an important paradox where sometimes patients may be empowered by giving a narrative account of their story, while others may feel anxiety from reliving those moments of their life. According to Grotcher and Edwards (1990), when participants used communication to reduce their fear of their illness, they were likely to communicate about their illness more often. Walker and Dickson (2004) show that narratives are important in understanding and meeting the expectations of the family members when they are chronically ill. Oftentimes people will have expectations for their family members without verbally expressing them, leaving family members more often than not confused about what direction to take. However, a narrative or forms of storytelling in the case of a chronic physical illness may reflect some of the patients' unfulfilled needs and help family members to identify them.

Chronic Mental Illness

A chronic mental illness can be extremely hard for families to cope with given the negative social stigmas that exist about the illness in most societies around the world today. A chronic mental illness in a family member could lead to almost constant care and monitoring, depending upon the illness and the intensity. Families may find it difficult to cope with or come to terms with a family member's diagnosis of a chronic mental illness due to the many challenges it presents. Much of the literature surrounding mental illness in the family is psychology-based, and there is a strong need for communication-based studies to better understand these unique families.

Marriage. An important aspect of the family dynamic is marriage. It is the foundation of most families and gives people feelings of stability. Communication is essential to marriage, but little literature exists exploring the communication around a diagnosis of a mental illness. However, much literature exists on its effects on marriage. Perry (2014) focused on social networks and stigma in relation to those with a serious mental illness. A spouse is a very prominent and strong part of a married person's social network. If someone is entering or exiting a marriage, that person's social network changes in many different ways. Perry (2014) found that the stigma of a mental illness had contact with the social network, and the relationship between the two works ambiguously together, meaning that the social network responded to the mental illness through their own thinking, and proving that spouses typically control family conversations. Spouses decide the climate of the family views and values toward different topics as they raise their offspring, if they choose to have any. Segrin (2006) shows that there is a strong call for communication scholars to explore the way that families interact, especially about mental illness, and that a positive or a negative attitude can set a precedent for what future family communication will be like based on how spouses interact. The different communication processes that couples partake of set examples for children's interaction. Adding mental illness to the mixture, Schmaling and Jacobson (1990) show that wives who are depressed are more likely to make an aggressive comment to their husbands than wives who are not depressed and that depressed wives have fewer positive discussions than their counterparts. These aggressive statements could likely become a stressor for the marriage or produce a negative schemata of marriage for children or adolescents in the family. Segrin (2006) offers that depression has a large impact on the family and usually just creates more problems, tending to result in fueling depression. However this assertion could also be true of the communication patterns surrounding many other types of mental illnesses in the family.

Parent–Child. As regards the parent–child relationship in reference to mental illnesses, it is known that parents are the primary caregivers to children and adolescents with chronic mental illnesses. Literature mainly focuses on the illness from the parents' perspective, rather than the child's, suggesting that little is known about children's perceptions of the parents' mental illnesses. Richardson, Cobham, McDermott, and Murray (2013) explained that parents' feelings of loss about an adult child with a mental illness focus on grieving about ambiguous losses, like the child's loss of self or identity. This loss and grieving process has the potential to shape the family's behaviors and patterns of communications. Since there are usually no tangible effects of a mental illness, parents may often find it hard to cope with a diagnosis and come to terms with it. Even harder for families to process is the fact that in most cultures and societies in the world, there is a negative social stigma to having a mental illness. Richardson et al. (2013) also noted that parental grief over the child's mental illness was not socially acceptable. Several studies (Chadda, 2014; Richardson,

Cobham, McDermott, & Murray, 2013) discussed this notion that parents felt as though the illness or their own grief should be hidden because it is not socially acceptable. Most of the struggles that parents in this situation face are with the topics of self-concepts and identities, with variance to whether it is their own or their child's. Richardson et al. (2013) found that the child's illness changed the parents' own identity. Since the identity and self are such fluid concepts, it is important to understand the self and different identities as well as the changes that occur with the two in accordance with both the parents and the children. There is little literature in regard to mental health's effects on self-concepts and identities. Aside from the self, another important factor to contend with when discussing mental illness between the parents and children is parenting styles' effects on these children with mental illnesses. Hamond and Schrodt (2012) explored the effects of the different parenting styles on children's mental health and concluded that there was no statistically significant evidence that the different styles had an effect on mental health. However, Hamond and Schrodt (2012) continued by noting that findings indicated that acts of affection and authority make limited, but important, improvements to the child's mental health. When it is the parent in the relationship who is mentally ill, the communication process is entirely different, as found in Van Loon, Van de Ven, Van Doesum, Witteman, and Hosman (2014), where adolescents' internalizing and externalizing behaviors were correlated to parents' mental illness. Parents with mental illnesses were found to have a negative effect on the adolescent or child, the whole family, and even the parent and child's interactions (Van Loon, Van de Ven, Van Doesum, Witteman, & Hosman, 2014). This literature exemplifies that parental mental illness controls more channels of communication than a child or adolescent's mental illness does. While much literature exists about families and mental illness, unfortunately very few scholars focus on the talk that occurs about the family member with the illness, and the communication around this topic.

Reviewing the literature leads back to the question: How are those with a chronic illness treated by their families since their diagnosis? Analyzing both mental and physical illnesses and the family communication processes around them is essential to furthering the conversation that communication scholars are creating to understand these unique families.

REFERENCES ●━━━━━━━━━━━━━━━●

Badr, H., & Acitelli, L. K. (2005). Dyadic adjustment in chronic illness: Does relationship talk matter? *Journal of Family Psychology, 19*(3), 465–469. doi:10.1037/0893-3200.19.3.465

Berg, C. A., & Upchurch, R. (2007). A developmental-contextual model of couples coping with chronic illness across the adult life span, *Psychological Bulletin. 133*(6), 920–954.

Chadda, R. K. (2014). Caring for the family caregivers of persons with mental illness. *Indian Journal of Psychiatry, 56*(3), 221–227. doi:10.4103/0019-5545.140616

Freeman, E. M., & Couchonnal, G. (2006). Narratives and culturally based approaches in practices with families. *The Journal of Contemporary Social Services, 43*(3), 198–208.

Grotcher, J. M., & Edwards, R. (1990). Coping strategies of cancer patients: Actual communication and imagined interactions. *Health Communication, 2*, 255–266.

Hamond, J. D., & Schrodt, P. (2012). Do parental styles moderate the association between family conformity orientation and young adults' mental well-being? *The Journal of Family Communication, 12*, 151–166. doi:10.1080/15267431.2011.561149

Keyton, J. (2011). *Communication research: Asking questions, finding answers.* New York, NY: McGraw Hill.

Lorde, A. (1980). *The cancer journals.* San Francisco, CA: Sheba.

Ott Anderson, J., & Geist Martin, P. (2003). Narratives and healing: Exploring one family's stories of cancer survivorship. *Health Communication, 15*(2), 133–143.

Perry, B. L. (2013). Symptoms, stigma, or secondary social disruption: Three mechanisms of network dynamics in severe mental illness. *Journal of Social and Personal Relationships, 31*(1), 32–53. doi:10.1177/0265407513484632

Richardson, M., Cobham, V., McDermott, B., & Murray, J. (2013). Youth mental illness and the family: Parents' loss and grief. *Journal of Child and Family Studies, 22*, 719–736. doi:10.1007/s10826-012-9625-x

Rosland, A. (2009). Sharing the care: The role of family in chronic illness. *California Healthcare Foundation*, 1–27. Retrieved from https://www.chcf.org/publication/sharing-the-care-the-role-of-family-in-chronic-illness/

Schmaling, K. B., & Jacobson, N. S. (1990). Marital interaction and depression. *Journal of Abnormal Psychology*, *99*, 229–236.

Segrin, C. (2006). Family interactions and well-being: integrative perspectives. *The Journal of Family Communication*, *6*(1), 3–21.

Shuff, J., & Sims, J. D. (2013). Communication perceptions related to life-threatening illness in a relationship: A Q methodology study. *Florida Communication Journal*, *41*(2), 81–96.

Van Loon, L. M. A., Van de Ven, M. O. M., Van Doesum, K. T. M., Witteman, C. L. M., & Hosman, C. M. H. (2014). The relation between parental mental illness and adolescent mental health: The role of family factors. *Journal of Child and Family Studies*, *23*, 1201–1214. doi:10.1007/s10826-013-9781-7

Walker, K. L., & Dickson F. C. (2004). An exploration of illness-related narratives in marriage: The identification of illness-identity scripts. *Journal of Social and Personal Relationships*, *21*(4), 527–544. doi:10.1177/0265407504044846

Ward, B. W., Schiller, J. S., & Goodman, R. A. (2014). Multiple chronic conditions among U.S. adults: A 2012 update. *Preventing Chronic Disease*, *11*, doi: 10.5888/pcd11.130389

Index